**BRITISH RAILWAYS
PAST and PRESENT**

*Travelling
Companion*

No 1

KING'S CROSS: A scene typical of the LNER 'streamliner' era with two 'A4' streamlined locomotives standing in the great train sheds with a typical LNER signal box presiding over the operation. Pride of place is taken by No 2512 *Silver Fox* setting off with the 5.30 pm 'Silver Jubilee' service to Newcastle. The locomotive, which carries a fox emblem above the valances, is in Garter blue, although its train is in a silver-grey finish. To the right No 4495 *Golden Fleece*, on the 5.45 pm departure, will take 85 minutes longer to get to Newcastle.

In the 1993 view there is less track on the ground but a lot of overhead equipment in the air. Class '47/4' No 47833 in original green livery sets off on 28 January with the 12.20 ARPS special to Peterborough after being named *Captain Peter Manisty RN*. *E. R. Wethersett/BM*

BRITISH RAILWAYS PAST and PRESENT

Travelling Companion

No 1

The East Coast Main Line

King's Cross to Newcastle

Geoffrey Body
Principal photographer Brian Morrison

Based on *Mile by Mile on the LNER*
by
S. N. Pike MBE

Silver Link Publishing Ltd

Companion with this volume
Britain's Rail Routes Past and Present
THE EAST COAST MAIN LINE
King's Cross to Newcastle: the route of the 'Silver Jubilee'
Geoffrey Body
Principal photographer Brian Morrison
Foreword by Brian Burdsall, Managing Director, InterCity East Coast Ltd
Over 350 'past and present' photographs and maps provide a detailed portrait of six
decades of one of Britain's premier rail routes.
ISBN 1 85794 052 0

Also available
LNER REFLECTIONS
A collection of photographs from the Hulton Picture Company
Edited by Nigel Harris
Foreword by the Earl of Lichfield
Superb press photographs of the LNER in the 1920s and '30s.
ISBN 0 947971 03 3

Errata from the original 1947 edition
Map 14: The true position of mileposts 165, 166 and 167 is slightly north of where
indicated on this map, milepost 167 being north of the Goole Canal, not south of the
bridge as shown.
Map 16: The correct name of the Junction 2 miles north of York is Skelton Junct, not
Poppleton as shown.

This edition © Silver Link Publishing Ltd
1995

Maps and other facsimiled material first
published by Atlas Publishing Company in
1947 in *Mile by Mile on the LNER: Kings
Cross Edition* by S. N. Pike MBE, and
facsimiled by Silver Link Publishing Ltd
in 1988

With thanks to Nick Dodson

First published in September 1995

British Library Cataloguing in Publication
Data

A catalogue record for this book is available
from the British Library

ISBN 1 85794 075 X

Silver Link Publishing Ltd
Unit 5, Home Farm Close
Church Street
Wadenhoe
Peterborough PE8 5TE
Tel/fax (01832) 720440

Printed and bound in Great Britain

Contents

Publisher's note

1995 marks both the 60th anniversary of the introduction of the 'Silver Jubilee' between Newcastle and London, Britain's first streamlined express train service, and the 10th anniversary of Silver Link Publishing, named after one of the four Class 'A4' 'Pacific' streamlined locomotives built to haul the new service. To mark the event Silver Link and Past & Present are publishing a range of books exploring the past and present of the celebrated East Coast Main Line, of which this is one (the others are listed opposite). Drawing together the fascinating maps from S. N. Pike's original 1947 book, a selection of photographs from the principal anniversary volume and a detailed commentary by Geoffrey Body describing the changes wrought by 60 years of railway development, this is the ideal travelling companion for any journey on today's East Coast Main Line.

A brief history of the East Coast Main Line

The first effective rail services from London to Edinburgh via the East Coast route were complicated and exhausting. The Great Northern Railway's line from London to near Peterborough had been open since 1850, and work on the 'Towns Line' thence through Grantham was making progress, but for another two years passengers had to travel via Boston and Lincoln to Retford. From Doncaster to York the journey was via the Lancashire & Yorkshire Railway to Knottingley, then the York & North Midland Railway. The Great North of England Railway had opened from York to Darlington in 1841, whence the Newcastle & Darlington Junction Railway cobbled together a link to the Tyne from 1844, which was permanently bridged from 1849.

The 'Towns Line' between Peterborough and Retford opened in 1852, and by 1860 there was a regular through King's Cross-Edinburgh train leaving London using jointly owned stock; this became the 'Special Scotch Express' from 1862, forerunner of the legendary 'Flying Scotsman'. Departing at 10 am and spending 20 minutes at York while passengers consumed a hurried meal, the train took 10½ hours to reach Edinburgh.

Following the completion of agreements between the GNR, NER and NBR in 1854, the line from King's Cross to Scotland began to be seen as a single entity. By 1860 there were plans for joint stock and through express services; the 10½-hour schedule improved to 9, then to 8½ after the 1888 'Race to Edinburgh' showed what was possible. As the new century dawned, timings generally remained at 8¼ hours or more as heavier loads consumed the dividends produced by larger engines. Through trains changed engines at Grantham, York and Newcastle.

The early 1920s saw the introduction of the first of Nigel Gresley's 'Pacifics', which enabled the newly formed London & North Eastern Railway to usher in the true express era. The 'Flying Scotsman' got a new train in 1924, including Gresley's new articulated dining cars with electric cooking. In July 1927 came the first of the new improved 'A1s', reclassified 'A3'. In the same month non-stop services began between King's Cross and Newcastle, followed later by Edinburgh. Gresley's innovative corridor tender allowed a crew changeover *en route* without having to stop the train. For the inaugural run on 1 May 1928 No 4472 *Flying Scotsman* reached Edinburgh in 8 hrs 2 mins. By the end of the season the train, with its cocktail bar, ladies' retiring room, hairdressing saloon and W. H. Smith newsman, had carried nearly 40,000 passengers.

Gresley's new 'A3' 'super-Pacifics' arrived in 1928 and set the stage for a new period of express passenger train achievement. New speed records were being established abroad, and in 1934 Gresley sampled Germany's streamlined 'Fliegende Hamburger'. Test runs between London and Leeds followed, using a light steam-hauled train rather than the preferred continental diesel option, and in March 1935 a six-coach train set a new record of 108 mph.

Then on 27 September 1935 came the press launch of Britain's first streamlined train, the 'Silver Jubilee', with its seven luxuriously furnished, silver-grey alloy articulated coaches. Behind *Silver Link*, the first of the streamlined 'A4' 'Pacifics', the train ran at over 100 mph all the way from Hatfield to Huntingdon, and set up a new 112½ mph record. The public service began on 30 September with a 4 hour up journey leaving Newcastle at 10 am and returning at 5.30 pm, both with a stop at Darlington.

On 27 August 1936 No 2512 *Silver Fox* with the 'Silver Jubilee' established a new record with a speed of 113 mph, but in June 1937 the LMS claimed 114 mph, to which the LNER responded with a trial run of its new 'Coronation' service, but could only manage 109½ mph. However, the new service, with its observation saloon and haulage by brand new 'A4' 'Pacifics', was an immediate success, and a third 'Coronation' set was allocated to a new streamlined 'West Riding Limited'.

Braking capacity was now the main factor inhibiting speed. On 3 July 1938 No 4468 *Mallard* was booked for a brake trial with a load of 'Coronation' vehicles plus dynamometer car; Sir Nigel Gresley himself was on board. Down Stoke Bank, south of Grantham, *Mallard* accelerated to a fraction over 126 mph, with 5 miles at 120.4 mph, a record that has never been beaten.

The streamliners were withdrawn at the outbreak of war in 1939 and the LNER concentrated on carrying massive quantities of freight and strategic materials. Emerging from the war grimy and worn, the LNER was determined to rebuild; by 1946 it had published *Forward*, a £90 million plan for rejuvenating the system, including many proposed improvements along the East Coast Main Line.

However, despite these grand plans the infrastructure of the ECML remained generally little changed with the exception of a few wartime additions and the slow post-war maintenance recovery. Then, at last, 1952 brought the first signs of real change with approval for two extra tracks in the Potters Bar area. This was also a period of freight acceleration, including a non-stop run to York for the 15.15 Scotch Goods from King's Cross. In 1956 the new 'Talisman' service took up the old 'Coronation' path to Edinburgh, while 1957 saw the appearance of the first diesel locomotives. On 21 June 1958 D201 worked the down 'Flying Scotsman' to Newcastle, the first scheduled working of an inter-city service by diesel traction.

With an order placed for 22 English Electric 'Deltics', the ECML traction scene was changing at last. However, passed over for electrification in favour of the West Coast route, the ECML suffered a period of low morale and indifferent services; there were problems with the new diesels, and disruption resulting from the improvement works.

In 1961 the first of the 'Deltics' arrived, and by the end of the summer the 'A4s' had worked their last non-stop ECML service. The era of high-speed timetabling began in earnest on 18 June 1962; the 'Deltic'-hauled 'Tees-Tyne Pullman' recorded the first ever start-to-stop timing of more than 75 mph. In 1963 the 'A4s' finally bowed out, and steam ended altogether on Christmas Eve two years later.

The whole character of the East Coast Main Line was now changing; more paths became available for passenger trains, and there were steady improvements in the permanent way. By the beginning of 1967 the 100 mph signs applied to 77 miles of the route from King's Cross to Edinburgh.

May 1968 saw the full implementation of fast and frequent services using

'Deltics' hauling only eight coaches, an idea owing much to the earlier 'Silver Jubilee' and 'Coronation' services; there was a moment of nostalgia when a train hauled by No 4472 *Flying Scotsman* commemorated the 40th anniversary of non-stop running to Edinburgh.

As the 1970s began, over half the distance to Newcastle was to the 95/100 mph standard, the King's Cross-Sandy resignalling scheme was approved and Mark IId air-conditioned coaches came into service. In addition the Government approved the GN suburban electrification proposals. By 1976 89% of the route was up to 100 mph standards.

Then in 1973 the prototype High Speed Train heralded a new dawn by recording 143.2 mph between York and Darlington. Further improvements provided the HSTs with a 125 mph trackbed, and modern signalling was extended north to Doncaster. Suburban electric services reached Royston from Moorgate in 1978, by which time the production HSTs were being delivered; eight 125 mph services appeared in the May timetable, among them the 'Flying Scotsman', which reached Edinburgh in less than 5 hours. In 1979 the 'Deltics' were relegated to lesser services, and withdrawals had commenced; HSTs were getting to York in 111 minutes, an average of 101.8 mph.

In 1983 the Selby Diversion created an entirely new section of main line to release the area north of Selby for a vast new coalfield. The following year approval was granted for the £306 million electrification of the ECML to Edinburgh, already being reached in 4½ hours.

On 27 September 1985 an HST special broke the world long-distance diesel traction record by covering 268.6 miles at an average of 115.4 mph, with a top speed of 144 mph; however, by November electrification work was sufficiently advanced for local services to work through to Huntingdon, and six months later to Peterborough. Leeds came 'under the wires' in 1988, York in 1989, Northallerton in mid-1990 and finally 'Intercity 225' reached Edinburgh in June 1991. Service improvements were accompanied by major remodelling schemes at Newcastle and York. On 26 September 1991 a light train hauled by No 91012 averaged 112.9 mph to Edinburgh, while on 2 June 1995 No 91031 set a new record of 155 mph.

Today the East Coast Main Line is Britain's premier rail route, providing a speed and quality of service that even the go-ahead Directors of the GNR and LNER would not have believed possible.

Author's Note

The pleasures and thrills of the journey between Kings Cross and Edinburgh are limitless. Every mile of the trip embraces some special feature of interest or beauty to compel the attention of the passenger.

The object of this little book is to encourage the passenger to anticipate his progress, and to enable him to know, to a nicety, what he next will see from the window at any and every stage of the journey. It is such a pity to sacrifice this experience to idle slumber, or to concentration on a magazine that would the better be enjoyed at home.

The beautiful countryside rushes by; beneath the tranquil surface, right beside the line, miners are toiling for the black diamonds essential to feed the great industrial plants we pass.

I acknowledge, with grateful thanks, certain information given me by Officials of the L.N.E.R. Railwaymen of every grade have contributed their share to make this publication as complete as possible. Railwaymen are justly proud of the vast organisation they serve; it is their wish that passengers should enjoy to the full the journeys they make with such speed and safety. The information and advice they have so readily placed at my disposal has been gladly offered with that end in view.

Shepperton, 1947.   S. N. P.

LONDON—EDINBURGH

COLUMN 4 TO BE FILLED IN BY PASSENGER

EXACT DISTANCES BETWEEN STATIONS—EXPRESS TRAIN RUNNING-TIMES

(1) STATION	(2) Distance Between Stations		(3) Express Train Running Times	(4) Actual Running Times			(5) NOTES and Average Speeds over each Section
	Miles	Yards	Minutes	Minutes	Early	Late	
KING'S CROSS to HATFIELD	17	1,199	27				From a standing start the heavily laden express encounters a severe 1 : 107 gradient through the Gasworks and Copenhagen tunnels, to be followed by a steep 1 : 200 climb for 8 miles from milepost 4 to Potters Bar, where the summit is reached. From here we rush through Hatfield at really high speed. *Average speed 39.0 m.p.h.*, the low figure being due to the difficult start.
HATFIELD to HITCHIN	14	424	14				The summit on this section is at Woolmer Green Box, near milepost 24. The junction of the lines at Langley are passed at 65 to 70 m.p.h. Water is taken on at the Troughs at milepost 27 at this speed, which we maintain through Hitchin. *Average speed 61 m.p.h.*
HITCHIN to HUNTINGDON	26	1,672	26				This is a really fast section of the line, and, except for a slowing down for curves near Offord, a very high speed is maintained. *Average speed 62.3 m.p.h.*
HUNTINGDON to PETERBOROUGH	17	863	19				An exceptionally fast section of the line. The necessity for approaching Peterborough at a minimum pace reduces our average speed to 55.2 m.p.h.
PETERBOROUGH to GRANTHAM	29	165	44				From a standing start at Peterborough we encounter a series of rising gradients from milepost 85 for the next 15 miles. Over the summit we pass through Great Ponton at very high speed, slowing down slightly for Grantham. *Average speed 39.5 m.p.h.*
GRANTHAM to NEWARK	14	1,138	14				Very high speeds are attained on the falling gradients. *Average over the section 63.2 m.p.h.*
NEWARK to RETFORD	18	902	24				Between Newark and milepost 128 the line is dead level, but rising gradients up to Askham tunnel lower the average. Speed is sharply reduced approaching Retford. *Average speed 46.2 m.p.h.*

COLUMN 4 TO BE FILLED IN BY PASSENGER

LONDON—EDINBURGH

EXACT DISTANCES BETWEEN STATIONS—EXPRESS TRAIN RUNNING TIMES

(1)	(2)		(3)	(4)			(5)
STATION	Distance Between Stations		Express Train Running Times	Actual Running Times			NOTES and Average Speeds over each Section
	Miles	Yards	Minutes	Minutes	Early	Late	
RETFORD to DONCASTER	17	611	19				Falling gradients approaching Scrooby water-troughs send us over the water pick-up at 65 m.p.h. The line rises steeply to milepost 150, but we again make fine speed to the outskirts of Doncaster. Average speed 55.2 m.p.h.
DONCASTER to YORK	32	308	42				The 6 miles of level track between mileposts 158 and 166 is a high speed section, and well worth "clocking." We slow down for the curve and swing bridge at Selby and also for the curve at Chaloner's Whin Junction. The sharp curve at York is approached slowly. Average speed 46.0 m.p.h.
YORK to THIRSK	22	352	25				12 miles of dead level and dead straight track allows for really fast travelling. By the time we reach Tollerton, speeds are in excess of 75 m.p.h. The standing start at York, however, reduces our average to 53.4 m.p.h.
THIRSK to NORTHALLERTON	7	1,320	8				The line rises very slightly. This section is covered at an average of 58.1 m.p.h.
NORTHALLERTON to DARLINGTON	14	308	15				The Wiske Water-troughs are taken at high speed. Speed is reduced approaching Darlington and we average 57.0 m.p.h. over this 14½ miles.
DARLINGTON to FERRY HILL	12	1,496	16				The line rises 1 : 220 and 1 : 203 until we reach the summit by milepost 55, 252 feet above sea level. We average 47.4 m.p.h. over this section.
FERRY HILL to DURHAM	9	330	12				Severe rising and falling gradients and speed restrictions limit our speed on this section, and we average 46.2 m.p.h.
DURHAM to NEWCASTLE	14	66	19				This is not a fast section of the line and our average works out at 44.2 m.p.h. The approach to Newcastle over the King Edward Bridge is taken very slowly.

11

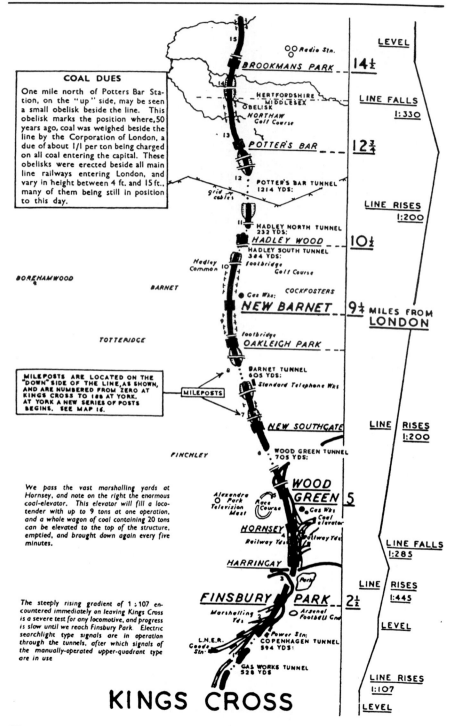

COAL DUES

One mile north of Potters Bar Station, on the "up" side, may be seen a small obelisk beside the line. This obelisk marks the position where, 50 years ago, coal was weighed beside the line by the Corporation of London, a due of about 1/1 per ton being charged on all coal entering the capital. These obelisks were erected beside all main line railways entering London, and vary in height between 4 ft. and 15 ft., many of them being still in position to this day.

MILEPOSTS ARE LOCATED ON THE "DOWN" SIDE OF THE LINE, AS SHOWN, AND ARE NUMBERED FROM ZERO AT KINGS CROSS TO 188 AT YORK. AT YORK A NEW SERIES OF POSTS BEGINS. SEE MAP 16.

We pass the vast marshalling yards at Hornsey, and note on the right the enormous coal-elevator. This elevator will fill a loco-tender with up to 9 tons in one operation, and a whole wagon of coal containing 20 tons can be elevated to the top of the structure, emptied, and brought down again every five minutes.

The steeply rising gradient of 1 : 107 encountered immediately on leaving Kings Cross is a severe test for any locomotive, and progress is slow until we reach Finsbury Park. Electric searchlight type signals are in operation through the tunnels, after which signals of the manually-operated upper-quadrant type are in use

LEVEL

BROOKMANS PARK — 14½

LINE FALLS 1:330

POTTER'S BAR — 12¾

LINE RISES 1:200

HADLEY WOOD — 10½

NEW BARNET — 9¼ MILES FROM LONDON

OAKLEIGH PARK

NEW SOUTHGATE — LINE RISES 1:200

WOOD GREEN — 5

HORNSEY

LINE FALLS 1:285

HARRINGAY

FINSBURY PARK — 2½ LINE RISES 1:445

LEVEL

LINE RISES 1:107

KINGS CROSS

LEVEL

King's Cross to Brookmans Park

Deriving its name from a monument to King George IV, the King's Cross terminus of the East Coast Main Line was opened in 1852 on the site of an old fever hospital, replacing an 1850 temporary station at Maiden Lane. Austere but well-loved, King's Cross retains the original double-span train shed and Italianate clock tower, but the supplementary layout has changed greatly since LNER days. A frontal extension has helped to modernise ticketing, information and interchange, while at the station 'throat' the track layout has been dramatically simplified to reduce conflicting movements and their potential for delay.

The dirt, grime and magic (!) of the steam locomotive shed (on the down/northbound side of the line north of Gasworks Tunnel) have gone, along with the line through York Road to Moorgate and the notorious Hotel Curve up again. A host of former signal boxes in the area have been replaced by one modern signalling panel (on the up/southbound side), which controls the whole route as far as Sandy.

Today's InterCity 125 and 225 trains and the local services from the modernised suburban station make light of the climb through the Gasworks and Copenhagen tunnels, and one bore of each has become redundant. Further up Holloway Bank another change has been the conversion of the former flyover leading to King's Cross Goods into one carrying the Up Slow line to the suburban side of the station.

Approaching Finsbury Park, Arsenal's Highbury ground is still visible (up) but housing has replaced the former diesel depot (down), once home of the Class 55 'Deltic' locomotives that did so much for the East Coast Main Line's reputation. At the station the one-time services to Broad Street and the Northern Heights have been exchanged for Class 313 electric multiple units (EMUs), which run over the old Great Northern & City line to Moorgate and change from 25kV AC overhead traction to 750V DC third rail for the tunnel section. Cambridge and

---

Opening and closing dates

Main line - opened from Maiden Lane temporary terminus to Peterborough 7.8.1850; King's Cross opened 14.10.1852.

King's Cross-Moorgate - regular service to Farringdon Street from 1.10.1863, extended to Moorgate 23.12.1865. Additional 'Widened Lines' into passenger use 17.2.1868. York Road station and Hotel Curve closed 8.11.1976 with introduction of Moorgate service via GN&C line from Finsbury Park.

Finsbury Park-Moorgate (GN&C) - opened 14.2.1904, to Metropolitan Railway 1.7.1913.

Finsbury Park-Broad Street - passenger trains over Canonbury spur from 18.1.1875, ended with GN suburban electrification.

Finsbury Park-Edgware - opened 22.8.1867; to High Barnet 1.4.1872; both lines to LT. Highgate to Alexandra Palace opened 24.5.1873, closed 5.7.1954.

Hertford Loop from Wood Green - opened to Enfield 26.4.1871, to Cuffley 4.4.1910, to Langley 4.3.1918 (goods), 2.6.1924 (passenger).

NEW BARNET: Although the track layout at New Barnet retains some similarities, every other aspect of these two photographs testifies to the dramatic changes of the last few decades. The LNER signal box has gone, along with the somersault signals and their attendant signal wire and point rodding, and even the telephone lines have disappeared from the poles in favour of fibre-optic cables in lineside ducts. Below the electric current wiring and structures the rails are now flat-bottomed and spiked to concrete sleepers instead of the traditional bullhead design in chairs on wooden sleepers. The proud trains have changed just as much, from one of the newly introduced 'Silver Jubilee' services on 16 July 1937 to a modern InterCity express on 19 August 1994.

In the first illustration the down 'Silver Jubilee' is headed by the streamlined Gresley 'A4' 'Pacific' No 2510 *Quicksilver*, while in the second the 15.00 King's Cross-Edinburgh service is powered by Class 91 No 91025 *BBC Radio 1 FM*. *John P. Wilson (Rail Archive Stephenson)/BM*

Peterborough trains also call at the simplified and modernised Finsbury Park and the station has additional underground services via the Victoria Line.

In place of Ferme Park up and down freight yards and Hornsey loco, the Harringay/Hornsey area now contains all the coach stabling, servicing and maintenance activity that once occupied every nook and cranny along the first few miles of the main line. West Anglia & Great Northern's Train Servicing Centre (up) is surrounded by siding accommodation linked by the flyover whose main function used to be the transfer of freight between the up and down yards.

Approaching Alexandra Palace, the palace itself is on the down side while opposite, just beyond where the 'Coronation' sets used to be serviced, is Bounds Green InterCity Depot, which takes care of the 31 locomotives and coach sets of the InterCity 225 fleet. The line to Hertford, started as a local branch and completed as a diversionary route for the main line, begins at this point, which was known as Wood Green before the revival of the 1873 Alexandra Palace building.

Along the main line, heading for New Barnet, the Standard Telephone Works building is still there (up) and still has telecommunications connections. Nowadays the inner suburban rail service has pushed further north as the commuter belt has expanded, and its trains have the benefit of a much improved section on the climb up to Potters Bar. In the 1950s the previous double track here was quadrupled in a scheme that provided an extra bore for each of the three tunnels and a rebuild for Hadley Wood and Potters Bar stations. Beyond the latter the 'Coal Dues' obelisk, as described by Pike in 1947, can still be spotted among the trees.

FERME PARK: Crossing over the main line between Harringay and Hornsey, Class 'J52/2' 0-6-0ST No 68846 heads a mixed freight for the North London line on 5 October 1957. This is still the era of the small wagon, with the Esso tanks at the front of the train followed by Conflats, then examples of Open and Boxvan types. In the adjoining Ferme Park up and down yards this incredible sort of mixture would be equally evident, together with all the other paraphernalia of moving goods traffic - brake vans, cattle pens, loading docks, load gauges, shunting poles, tail lamps and the like. Today the viaduct has been completely rebuilt and the track alignment altered, the present-day scene bearing little resemblance to this photograph. *Stanley Creer*

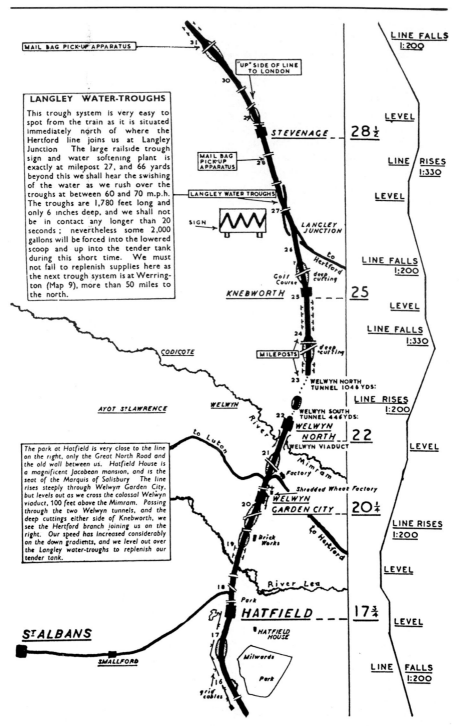

MAIL BAG PICK-UP APPARATUS

LINE FALLS
1:200

"UP" SIDE OF LINE
TO LONDON

LANGLEY WATER-TROUGHS

This trough system is very easy to spot from the train as it is situated immediately north of where the Hertford line joins us at Langley Junction. The large railside trough sign and water softening plant is exactly at milepost 27, and 66 yards beyond this we shall hear the swishing of the water as we rush over the troughs at between 60 and 70 m.p.h. The troughs are 1,780 feet long and only 6 inches deep, and we shall not be in contact any longer than 20 seconds; nevertheless some 2,000 gallons will be forced into the lowered scoop and up into the tender tank during this short time. We must not fail to replenish supplies here as the next trough system is at Werrington (Map 9), more than 50 miles to the north.

STEVENAGE — 28½

LEVEL

LINE / RISES
1:330

MAIL BAG
PICK-UP
APPARATUS

LANGLEY WATER TROUGHS

LEVEL

SIGN

LANGLEY
JUNCTION

to Hertford

Golf Course

deep cutting

LINE FALLS
1:200

KNEBWORTH — 25

LEVEL

LINE FALLS
1:330

CODICOTE

MILEPOSTS

deep cutting

WELWYN NORTH
TUNNEL 1046 YDS:

LINE RISES
1:200

AYOT St LAWRENCE

WELWYN

River

WELWYN SOUTH
TUNNEL 446 YDS:

WELWYN
NORTH — 22

LEVEL

WELWYN VIADUCT

to Luton

Mimram

Factory

The park at Hatfield is very close to the line on the right, only the Great North Road and the old wall between us. Hatfield House is a magnificent Jacobean mansion, and is the seat of the Marquis of Salisbury. The line rises steeply through Welwyn Garden City, but levels out as we cross the colossal Welwyn viaduct, 100 feet above the Mimram. Passing through the two Welwyn tunnels, and the deep cuttings either side of Knebworth, we see the Hertford branch joining us on the right. Our speed has increased considerably on the down gradients, and we level out over the Langley water-troughs to replenish our tender tank.

Shredded Wheat Factory

WELWYN
GARDEN CITY — 20¼

Brick Works

to Hertford

LINE RISES
1:200

LEVEL

River Lea

HATFIELD — 17¾

Park

LEVEL

St ALBANS

HATFIELD
HOUSE

SMALLFORD

Millwards

Park

LINE \ FALLS
1:200

grid cables

Welham Green to Stevenage

Making the point that the British rail system is no longer dominated by closures, this section starts with a new station. Welham Green, with its six-car platforms to the Slow lines, was opened in 1986 as a result of co-operation with and contributions from the local councils. Unlike some other main lines, the LNER laid its Slow lines outside the Fast or Main pair, rather than grouping them, and this allows stations such as Welham Green to be served without interfering with faster services.

Its neighbour, Hatfield, has lost its small loco shed and the modest branch line to St Albans, but has gained a modernised station and a car park for the commuters it draws from a wide area. Many are from the new town development that was grafted upon the earlier township, but Hatfield also has historic associations, not least from Hatfield House (up side), the 17th-century home of the Cecil family. The old station used to have a waiting room reserved for the use of Queen Victoria.

Welwyn Garden City station was also something of a latecomer to the railway scene. It opened in 1926 as one of the facilities of the new 'garden city' that sprang from the forward-looking ideas and actions of Sir Ebenezer Howard, the father of town planning. Today the station is an integral part of the Howard Centre that honours his name.

Trains used to run on two branch lines east and west of Welwyn Garden City, to Hertford and Dunstable respectively, and its up-side goods depot collected and delivered traffic over a wide area. Nowadays it is the passenger train service on the main line that is important, Welwyn Garden City being served by hourly trains to Peterborough and to Cambridge and by two originating services an hour to Moorgate. Carriage sidings and a flyover exist to help deal with the latter.

North of Welwyn Garden City the East Coast Main Line reduces from four tracks to two for its passage over the valley of the River Mimram and through a ridge of high ground beyond. The Welwyn or Digswell Viaduct, 519 yards long and with 40 arches up to 97 feet high, disposes of the first obstacle and, following Welwyn North station, two tunnels are used to penetrate the ridge and emerge at Woolmer Green where there is an emergency crossover and the Slow lines recommence.

The Hertford Loop rejoins the main line at Langley Junction, its down line

---

Opening and closing dates
Main line - Welham Green opened 29.9.1986, Welwyn Garden City 20 September 1926 and new Stevenage station 23.7.1973.
Hatfield-St Albans - opened 16.10.1865, closed 1.10.1951.
Hatfield-Dunstable - opened Luton-Dunstable 5.4.1858 (goods), 3.5.1858 (passengers), to Welwyn 1.9.1860; closed 26.4.1965.
Hatfield-Hertford - opened 1.3.1858, closed 18.6.1951.

WELWYN NORTH: The 'WD' locomotives were built in 1943 to a Riddles Ministry of Supply design labelled 'Austerity' because of its basic simplicity. They were purchased by the newly formed national railway system in 1948 and classified '8F'. Well over 700 were operational at one period, including No 90158 seen here passing Welwyn North on 17 April 1954 with a Class H freight from Ferme Park to Grantham.

Despite some cosmetic work Welwyn North 40 years later is still clearly a no-frills Great Northern station. The up-side staff building has a new roof, the platform a new seat and electricity has taken over from gas as well as steam, but there is no mistaking the origins of the station house, the footbridge and the platform canopy. The train is the 15.08 King's Cross-Cambridge semi-fast slowing for its stop on 14 October 1994 and formed of Class 317/2 No 317362. *Both BM*

burrowing beneath the main route to stay clear of its high-speed services. Where once steam railcars operated there is now an all-stations EMU service from Moorgate to Hertford and a semi-fast one on through Langley Junction to Letchworth. The water troughs and mail pick-up apparatus remarked upon by Pike in 1947 have both gone, but around a quarter of all Royal Mail letters are still moved by train, and Res (Rail Express Systems) operates 60 trains each day, many with TPO (Travelling Post Office) vehicles and others with 100 mph 'Super GUV' vehicles.

Knebworth, surrounded by the pleasant open, green countryside that is so typical of Hertfordshire, was the home of the offices that controlled main-line operation during the war period.

At Stevenage the original station further north closed in 1973 when the present one was opened to serve one of the first batch of new towns built to relieve congestion in Inner London. Now a number of main-line expresses call at Stevenage to provide a service to and from the North for local residents and business people and for those changing to the local EMU service.

HATFIELD: Helped by the down gradient of 1 in 200 from Welwyn Garden City, the up 'Flying Scotsman' passes through Hatfield at speed on 14 January 1978. The train is in the charge of Class 55 'Deltic' No 55012 *Crepello,* **carrying on the tradition of East Coast Main Line locomotives carrying the names of notable racehorses. On the section between Hatfield and Welwyn Garden City an extra single line on both the down and up sides used to carry the Dunstable and Hertford North trains (respectively), and these were operated as single lines rather than as adjuncts to the main line.** *BM*

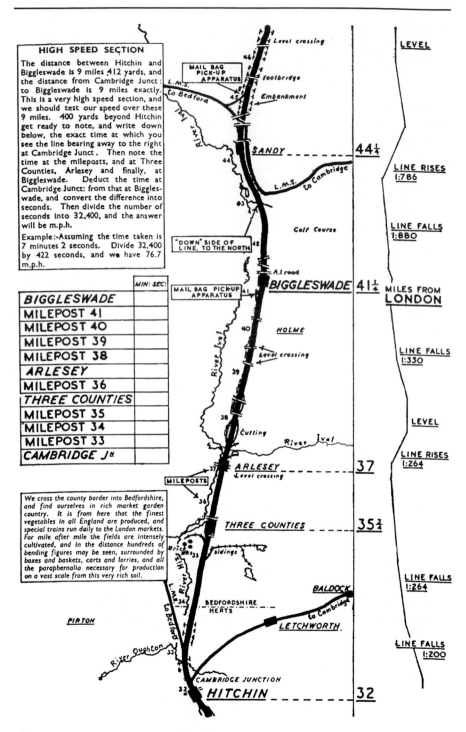

The distance between Hitchin and Biggleswade is 9 miles 412 yards, and the distance from Cambridge Junct. to Biggleswade is 9 miles exactly. This is a very high speed section, and we should test our speed over these 9 miles. 400 yards beyond Hitchin get ready to note, and write down below, the exact time at which you see the line bearing away to the right at Cambridge Junct. Then note the time at the mileposts, and at Three Counties, Arlesey and finally, at Biggleswade. Deduct the time at Cambridge Junct: from that at Biggleswade, and convert the difference into seconds. Then divide the number of seconds into 32,400, and the answer will be m.p.h.

Example:–Assuming the time taken is 7 minutes 2 seconds. Divide 32,400 by 422 seconds, and we have 76.7 m.p.h.

	MIN : SEC :
BIGGLESWADE	
MILEPOST 41	
MILEPOST 40	
MILEPOST 39	
MILEPOST 38	
ARLESEY	
MILEPOST 36	
THREE COUNTIES	
MILEPOST 35	
MILEPOST 34	
MILEPOST 33	
CAMBRIDGE Jⁿ	

We cross the county border into Bedfordshire, and find ourselves in rich market garden country. It is from here that the finest vegetables in all England are produced, and special trains run daily to the London markets. For mile after mile the fields are intensely cultivated, and in the distance hundreds of bending figures may be seen, surrounded by boxes and baskets, carts and lorries, and all the paraphernalia necessary for production on a vast scale from this very rich soil.

Level crossing

MAIL BAG PICK-UP APPARATUS

footbridge

L.M.S. to Bedford

Embankment

SANDY — — — — 44¼

L.M.S. to Cambridge

Golf Course

"DOWN" SIDE OF LINE, TO THE NORTH

A.1 road

MAIL BAG PICK-UP APPARATUS

BIGGLESWADE 41¼

HOLME

Level crossing

Cutting

River Ivel

ARLESEY — — — — 37
Level crossing

MILEPOSTS

THREE COUNTIES — — — 35¾

Brick Wks

sidings

BALDOCK

BEDFORDSHIRE HERTS

to Cambridge

PIRTON

LETCHWORTH

River Oughton

L.M.S. to Bedford

CAMBRIDGE JUNCTION

HITCHIN — — — — 32

LEVEL

LINE RISES 1:786

LINE FALLS 1:880

MILES FROM LONDON

LINE FALLS 1:330

LEVEL

LINE RISES 1:264

LINE FALLS 1:264

LINE FALLS 1:200

Hitchin to Sandy

Hitchin is important as the junction for the Cambridge line and is served by Cambridge and Peterborough Class 317 EMU trains along with the service from Moorgate to Letchworth. Its outer-suburban passengers are likely to be able to travel on new Class 365 'Networker Express' units from 1996 after the completion of minor station and other alterations along the two routes.

Before the line from Bedford to St Pancras was opened, Midland Railway trains reached London via Hitchin. The course of the old Bedford-Hitchin line they used is still discernible (down) but, like the former up-side loco shed, its active railway years are now but a memory. Hitchin has always had an extensive railway engineering activity but this has now transferred from the former up-side yard to the old goods yard area opposite.

Just north of Hitchin, past the surviving, modernised gas plant and a section of well-canted track, the River Hiz forms the boundary between Hertfordshire and Bedfordshire, and the rolling green fields of the former rapidly give way to a flat, arable landscape where corn and root crops thrive and are much in evidence. However, they are no longer rushed to the markets by express freight trains, their place being taken by steadily increasing passenger traffic now getting to London in times 25 per cent better than the best achievements of the past.

Three Counties and Arlesey lost their stations in 1959, but Arlesey regained its place on the railway map in 1988 with County, District and Parish councils contributing to the £630,000 cost of brand new platforms.

On its trial run on 27 September 1935 the 'Silver Jubilee' train reached 112½ mph behind the LNER's 'A4' Class streamlined 'Pacific' locomotive No 2509 *Silver Link* on the stretch of line between Arlesey and Biggleswade. That speed, remarkable as it was for the time, is now bettered as a matter of routine over this section where 125 mph is the norm.

Biggleswade, an old GN station with its stables still extant, also retains some business activity in its former goods yard. Sandy is similar but the location has been completely reconstructed. It once had two stations sharing a common central platform, one serving the Bletchley-Bedford-Cambridge line and the other the East Coast Main Line. With the closure of the former the opportunity was taken to get rid of the two-line bottleneck in the main line by using

---

Opening and closing dates
Main line - Three Counties and Arlesey closed 5.1.1959; latter reopened 1.10.1988.
Hitchin-Cambridge - opened to Royston 21.10.1850, to Shepreth 1.8.1851, to Cambridge 1.4.1852.
Hitchin-Bedford - opened 15.4.1857 (goods), 8.5.1857 (passengers), closed 1.1.1962.
Cambridge-Sandy-Bedford - Sandy-Potton opened by Captain Peel 23.6.1857, full route 7.7.1862; closed 1.1.1968.

SANDY used to be a bottleneck on the route north from King's Cross, the Down Slow section from Biggleswade ending under the wheels of Class 'A4' 'Pacific' No 60028 *Walter K. Whigham* in this photograph. Under clear signals the locomotive rushes a northbound express through the Bedfordshire junction in August 1960, making the most of this long, near-flat section of fertile agricultural land. The wagons in the goods yard appear to be cattle vans but, like Biggleswade, Sandy was noted for its market garden produce loadings and for the grain business of S. C. Banks.

The latter's silos can be seen in the second photograph, which also highlights the reconstruction from a two-track to a four-track section using space formerly occupied on the left by the Cambridge-Bedford line. On the Down Fast on 13 August 1994 Class 91 No 91029 *Queen Elizabeth II* has charge of the 18.00 King's Cross-Edinburgh InterCity service. *John C. Baker/BM*

the space released by the closed route to extend the four-track profile of the primary route.

Sandy is also the boundary between the King's Cross and Peterborough signalling control installations. Where many locations on the main line once had four, or even six, signal boxes, all manually operated, such installations have now been superseded by modern signalling centres that concentrate the safe and efficient management of points, signals and allied functions over a wide area at a single location. The latest Integrated Electronic Control Centres, in York and Tyneside, share control of the King's Cross- Newcastle route with the earlier centres at King's Cross, Peterborough and Doncaster.

North of Sandy there are more traces of the Cambridge-Bedford route (up), which started life as a local line built by Captain William Peel, son of the prime minister, and at one stage was scheduled to form part of a trunk rail route from East Anglia to South Wales. Light industry now occupies its course on one side of the main line, while the other is occupied by sandhills and the nearby headquarters of the Royal Society for the Protection of Birds.

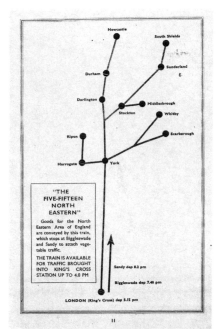

Right East Bedfordshire is a prominent market gardening area, and in steam days important northbound express freight services such as 'The Five-Fifteen North Eastern' made stops at Biggleswade and Sandy to pick up traffic.

Below SANDY: North of Sandy the former LMS line to Bedford became single track and continued that way almost to Bedford St Johns station. The bridge taking it across the East Coast Main Line is seen here on 1 January 1966 with a Cambridge-Oxford DMU. The ex-LNER and ex-LMS routes were formerly linked by a wartime spur. Today the secondary line has disappeared, leaving only its trackbed. The 'sandhills' on the right here were once a Roman settlement. *G. Body*

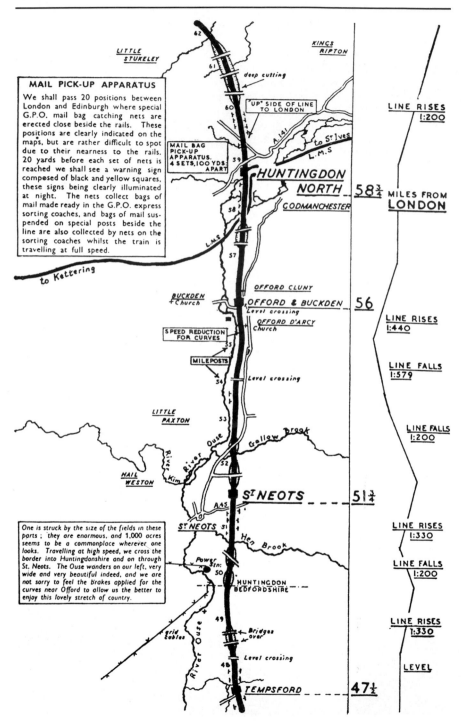

MAIL PICK-UP APPARATUS

We shall pass 20 positions between London and Edinburgh where special G.P.O. mail bag catching nets are erected close beside the rails. These positions are clearly indicated on the maps, but are rather difficult to spot due to their nearness to the rails. 20 yards before each set of nets is reached we shall see a warning sign composed of black and yellow squares, these signs being clearly illuminated at night. The nets collect bags of mail made ready in the G.P.O. express sorting coaches, and bags of mail suspended on special posts beside the line are also collected by nets on the sorting coaches whilst the train is travelling at full speed.

One is struck by the size of the fields in these parts; they are enormous, and 1,000 acres seems to be a commonplace wherever one looks. Travelling at high speed, we cross the border into Huntingdonshire and on through St. Neots. The Ouse wanders on our left, very wide and very beautiful indeed, and we are not sorry to feel the brakes applied for the curves near Offord to allow us the better to enjoy this lovely stretch of country.

LITTLE STUKELEY

KINGS RIPTON

deep cutting

'UP' SIDE OF LINE TO LONDON

MAIL BAG PICK-UP APPARATUS. 4 SETS,100 YDS. APART

HUNTINGDON NORTH _ _ **58¾** MILES FROM LONDON

GODMANCHESTER

to Kettering

BUCKDEN + Church

OFFORD CLUNY

OFFORD & BUCKDEN _ **56**
Level crossing

OFFORD D'ARCY Church

SPEED REDUCTION FOR CURVES

MILEPOSTS

Level crossing

LITTLE PAXTON

Gallow Brook

River Ouse

Kim

HAIL WESTON

St NEOTS _ _ _ **51¼**

A45

St NEOTS

Hen Brook

Power Stn:

HUNTINGDON
BEDFORDSHIRE

grid cables

River Ouse

Bridges over

Level crossing

TEMPSFORD _ _ _ **47½**

LINE RISES 1:200

LINE RISES 1:440

LINE FALLS 1:579

LINE FALLS 1:200

LINE RISES 1:330

LINE FALLS 1:200

LINE RISES 1:330

LEVEL

Tempsford to Huntingdon

For the next 10 miles or so the East Coast Main Line follows the course of the River Ouse, which is fed by brooks and streams from either side. The marauding Danes used the river for their inland incursions, but it is now the scene of more peaceful leisure boating pursuits with a least one holiday village on its banks. At Tempsford the river is still beyond the village itself, on the west side of the main line, while on the other side are the remaining traces of Tempsford aerodrome, used for clandestine wartime operations in the distant 1939-45 years but now returned to agriculture.

Tempsford station, once so busy with wartime supplies, is long closed and now marked only by some cottages and the level crossing, which is also much changed from its old form of traditional wooden gates controlled from the station signal box. Along the course of the main line such gates have given way to barriers (except at certain farm crossings), operated by track circuits or from distant locations under the control of TV camera systems. Warning to road traffic is given by flashing red lights.

Along the line to St Neots the traditional power generating station at Little Barford (down), now rebuilt, still retains a private siding connection, albeit little used. The main line, which has entered what used to be the county of Huntingdon, next comes to St Neots where the former Great Northern Railway station has been refurbished and, in addition to its two-trains-per-hour off-peak service has peak trains that cover the 51½ miles to King's Cross in only 43 minutes. Once a minor health resort, this market town was one of the last to abandon the tradition of coach links between railway station and local hotel. The Cross Keys Hotel was still running a small motor bus to and from the station, which is well east of the centre of the town, at the time that the *Mile by Mile* booklet was produced.

The main line joins the River Ouse beyond Little Paxton. Conforming to the river's course used to involve a speed restriction of 70 mph through the resulting curves and these 'Offord Curves' were something of a curse to railway operators and enginemen, losing them the speed advantages of the easier track sections on either side. However, an end to the problem was achieved in 1970 by easing the curves sufficiently to raise the maximum speed to 100 mph. This involved purchasing extra land to widen the trackbed, some strengthening and infilling of the river banks and adjusting the ancillary aspects of drainage, cabling and other supplementary features to the new track profile. With the river on one side (down) and

---

Opening and closing dates
Main line - Tempsford closed 5.11.1956, Offord & Buckden closed 2.2.1959.
Kettering-Huntingdon-Cambridge - opened Cambridge to Huntingdon 17.8.1847 and to Kettering 21.2.1866 (goods), 1.3.1866 (passengers); closed 15.6.1959.

SOUTH OF HUNTINGDON a couple of miles of level track precede a coming 3-mile rise at 1 in 200, and Gresley 'A3' 'Pacific' No 2578 *Bayardo* is pictured taking advantage of this to establish a good momentum for its heavy train. Built in 1924 as an 'A1' by the North British Locomotive Company, No 2578 was an early rebuild to 'A3' and worked in the latter form from 1928 to 1961.

In the modern view Class 91 No 91008 *Thomas Cook* works over the same stretch on 8 September 1994 in charge of the 15.00 King's Cross-Glasgow Central 'Scottish Pullman'. Below track level on the left is the course of the old Midland/LMS route from Kettering to Cambridge. *G. Body collection/BM*

three churches on the other, the Offord villages are now just a beauty spot and no longer a railway nightmare.

Huntingdon, where Oliver Cromwell was born in 1599, is approached by several bridges over the Ouse, which here turns east to add its charm to the townships of Godmanchester and St Ives. Although the station still uses its ex-Great Northern up-side buildings, the remainder has been remodelled and a car park occupies the site of the former Huntingdon East station (up), once serving the old line from Kettering to Cambridge, which passes under the ECML on its approach to Huntingdon, then rises on the east side. Huntingdon enjoys two services an hour to and from King's Cross, one of the workings turning round here.

OFFORD: Beyond Sandy the main line is joined by the River Ouse, the two being almost side by side between Little Paxton and Offord Cluny. This proximity produced curves in the railway necessitating speed restrictions, but these were eased under the Stage One round of improvements at the beginning of the 1970s. The proximity of railway and waterway shows well in this view of Class 91 No 91030 *Palace of Holyroodhouse* sweeping past with a northbound InterCity express from King's Cross on 20 August 1994. *Ken Brunt*

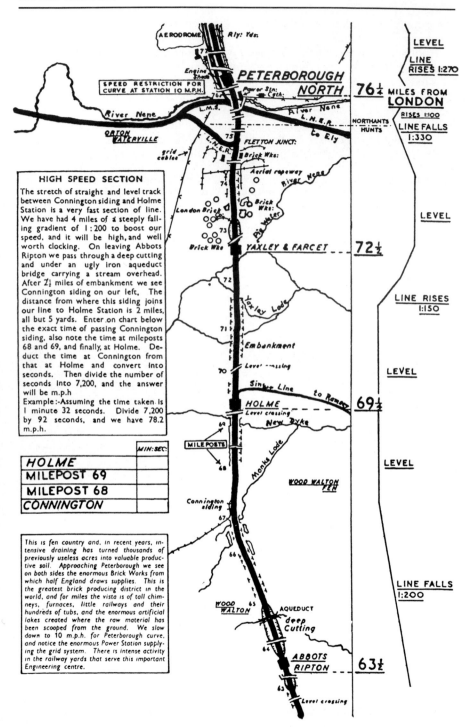

HIGH SPEED SECTION

The stretch of straight and level track between Connington siding and Holme Station is a very fast section of line. We have had 4 miles of a steeply falling gradient of 1 : 200 to boost our speed, and it will be high, and well worth clocking. On leaving Abbots Ripton we pass through a deep cutting and under an ugly iron aqueduct bridge carrying a stream overhead. After 2½ miles of embankment we see Connington siding on our left. The distance from where this siding joins our line to Holme Station is 2 miles, all but 5 yards. Enter on chart below the exact time of passing Connington siding, also note the time at mileposts 68 and 69, and finally, at Holme. Deduct the time at Connington from that at Holme and convert into seconds. Then divide the number of seconds into 7,200, and the answer will be m.p.h
Example :-Assuming the time taken is I minute 32 seconds. Divide 7,200 by 92 seconds, and we have 78.2 m.p.h.

	MIN: SEC:
HOLME	
MILEPOST 69	
MILEPOST 68	
CONNINGTON	

This is fen country and, in recent years, intensive draining has turned thousands of previously useless acres into valuable productive soil. Approaching Peterborough we see on both sides the enormous Brick Works from which half England draws supplies. This is the greatest brick producing district in the world, and for miles the vista is of tall chimneys, furnaces, little railways and their hundreds of tubs, and the enormous artificial lakes created where the raw material has been scooped from the ground. We slow down to 10 m.p.h. for Peterborough curve, and notice the enormous Power Station supplying the grid system. There is intense activity in the railway yards that serve this important Engineering centre.

Abbots Ripton to Peterborough

Some track simplification has taken place north of Huntingdon, but the climb up to the minor summit at Abbots Ripton is no longer the challenge it was in the days of steam traction.

Along the route there is a large air force base at Alconbury (down), but in essence this is a lonely stretch and the rescuers rushing to the scene of a three-train collision at Abbots Ripton in the winter of 1876 had a long and difficult way to come. In the accident 14 people lost their lives because the severity of the weather resulted in signals being frozen in the clear position instead of returning to danger. Mercifully today's colour light signals are immune to weather conditions and the position of trains is known at all times thanks to their occupation of track circuits showing on the signalling panel.

On the descent from the summit, past a lonely, isolated church (up), an engineer's tip area remains in use on the up side at Conington where there is also an emergency crossover. Little trace remains of the wartime marshalling yard that used to lie opposite and carried out work that would otherwise have been at risk from the bombing of New England yards at Peterborough.

Continuing its northward journey the line enters an area of rich, black fenland, now highly productive thanks to drainage work that started in this locality as early as 1639. At one time the drainage waterways were used for barging produce to the railway, but not only have the wharves largely disappeared but also the railway branches that dispossessed them. One such was the single line east from Holme to Ramsey, which lost its passenger trains in 1947 but stayed open for coal, potatoes and grain for some time after that. The old route can still be spotted (up) in its present guise as a farm track. It is followed on the east side of the line by Holme Fen, an area of silver birch trees that is also a nature reserve. To the west is the village of Stilton of cheese fame.

As the 1947 booklet indicates, each side of the line beyond the former Yaxley & Farcet station was once occupied by the pits, kilns and stacking areas of the numerous Fletton brickworks. A few visible but more distant works are still producing, but the lineside area is now almost empty of this once great hive of industry. The pits that yielded the highly-combustible clay have now gone, filled in with the help of an imaginative rail movement scheme that used up waste fuel ash from

---

Opening and closing dates

Main line - Abbots Ripton closed 15.9.1958, Holme closed 6.4.1959, Yaxley & Farcet closed 6.4.1959.

Holme-Ramsey North - opened 22.7.1863, closed 6.10.1947.

Peterborough-Northampton - opened 2.6.1845, closed 4.5.1964 (Rugby-Peterborough closed 6.6.1966).

Peterborough-Ely - opened 10.12.1846 (goods), 14.1.1847 (passengers).

Peterborough-Saxby - opened to Stamford 2.10.1846.

PETERBOROUGH: English Electric Type 4 (later Class 40) D350 is seen approaching Peterborough North station on 27 October 1962 hauling a King's Cross-York express. Crescent Junction signal box on the right controlled the link between the main line and the route up from Peterborough East. The original Peterborough North goods depot is on the left of the picture, while straight ahead lay Nene Sidings. Coaches stabled there on a cold winter's night were like travelling refrigerators to those catching early morning services, the steam heating frequently losing its battle with the riverside chill.

The second view graphically depicts the south-end remodelling at Peterborough. The main features of this were a new down island platform and through lines between this and the modified up-side facilities. On 13 August 1994 the 10.40 King's Cross-Edinburgh service, led by Class 91 No 91013 *Michael Faraday*, is leaving the Down Fast for No 4 Platform Line. The Down Slow can be seen crossing to the right to unite with the ex-MR Stamford line as far as Helpston. *Philip H. Wells/BM*

power stations and then covered this with top soil to allow normal cultivation. The main access route was via Fletton Junction (down), which also led to the sugar beet factory and the former railway line from Northampton and Rugby.

The East Coast Main Line has now reached the southern suburbs of Peterborough, and as it rises to cross the Ely line (up) and the River Nene there is a view of Fairground Meadow and the terminus of the Nene Valley Railway (down). This railway preservation scheme uses a section of the former Northampton line - the first railway to Peterborough - and operates a service with home and overseas steam locomotives through the area known as Nene Park. This development, along with many other worthwhile expansions and changes at Peterborough, have been prompted, aided or executed by the Peterborough Development Corporation, but at the heart of the city remains the beautiful cathedral, also visible from the train (up).

On the purely railway scene the changes at Peterborough have been dramatic. Its tired and grimy station and the dog-leg curve that brought train speeds down to a crawl have been transformed in a major remodelling and resignalling scheme of the 1970s. One of the main features of this was to provide well-aligned through tracks on which non-stop trains could pass through at up to 100 mph. An island platform was added on one side for down main line stopping services and those on the Stamford line, while the old station was altered and improved as a calling point for up trains. Just outside stands the Great Northern Hotel and just beyond that the entrance to the Queensway shopping centre.

HOLME: This view of Holme in Great Northern days is a reminder of the many wayside stations that the crack trains ignored and left to the humble and infrequent 'all-stations' services - 'parleys' as they were known to railwaymen. Holme also had a modest 5¾-mile branch east to Ramsey North, which survived a threat of omnibus replacement in the 1930s and struggled on until the LNER's own final year. Grain, potatoes and coal traffic then kept the branch open for freight for a few more years. *Lens of Sutton*

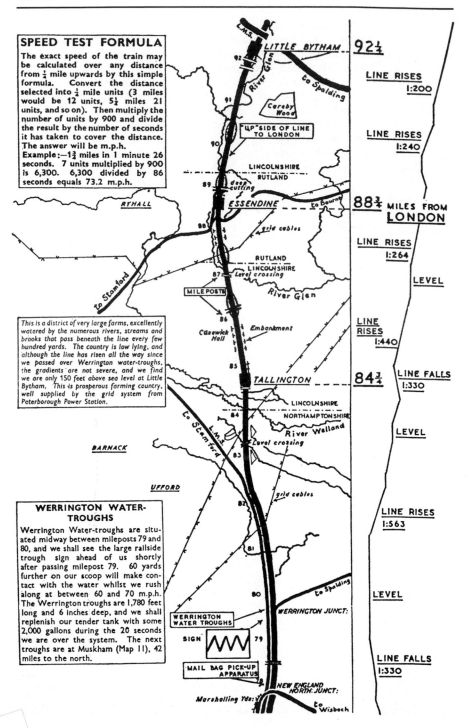

SPEED TEST FORMULA

The exact speed of the train may be calculated over any distance from ¼ mile upwards by this simple formula. Convert the distance selected into ¼ mile units (3 miles would be 12 units, 5¼ miles 21 units, and so on). Then multiply the number of units by 900 and divide the result by the number of seconds it has taken to cover the distance. The answer will be m.p.h.
Example:—1¾ miles in 1 minute 26 seconds. 7 units multiplied by 900 is 6,300. 6,300 divided by 86 seconds equals 73.2 m.p.h.

This is a district of very large farms, excellently watered by the numerous rivers, streams and brooks that pass beneath the line every few hundred yards. The country is low lying, and although the line has risen all the way since we passed over Werrington water-troughs, the gradients are not severe, and we find we are only 150 feet above sea level at Little Bytham. This is prosperous farming country, well supplied by the grid system from Peterborough Power Station.

WERRINGTON WATER-TROUGHS

Werrington Water-troughs are situated midway between mileposts 79 and 80, and we shall see the large railside trough sign ahead of us shortly after passing milepost 79. 60 yards further on our scoop will make contact with the water whilst we rush along at between 60 and 70 m.p.h. The Werrington troughs are 1,780 feet long and 6 inches deep, and we shall replenish our tender tank with some 2,000 gallons during the 20 seconds we are over the system. The next troughs are at Muskham (Map 11), 42 miles to the north.

L.M.S.

LITTLE BYTHAM **92¼**

to Spalding

LINE RISES
1:200

Careby Wood

"UP" SIDE OF LINE
TO LONDON

LINE RISES
1:240

LINCOLNSHIRE
RUTLAND
deep
cutting

RYHALL

ESSENDINE to Bourn **88¾** MILES FROM
LONDON

grid cables

LINE RISES
1:264

RUTLAND
LINCOLNSHIRE
Level crossing

LEVEL

MILE POST

River Glen

to Stamford

LINE
RISES
1:440

Casewick
Hall Embankment

TALLINGTON **84¾** LINE FALLS
1:330

LINCOLNSHIRE
NORTHAMPTONSHIRE
River Welland

LEVEL

BARNACK

to Stamford
L.M.S.
Level crossing

UFFORD

grid cables

LINE RISES
1:563

SIGN 79

to Spalding

LEVEL

WERRINGTON
WATER TROUGHS
WERRINGTON JUNCT:

MAIL BAG PICK-UP
APPARATUS

LINE FALLS
1:330

NEW ENGLAND
NORTH JUNCT:
Marshalling Yds:
to
Wisbech

Peterborough to Little Bytham

Before the advent of the Development Corporation, Peterborough was a railway town, nowhere more evident than in the area to the north of the station which was dominated by the New England marshalling yard and loco depot. Much of the traffic handled was coal on its way to the south, but the whole of the remaining up-side area is now devoted to the stabling of electrification stock and other permanent way or railway civil engineering activity. The Midland & Great Northern Joint line to Wisbech and Kings Lynn used to cross the main line here, but now only the ECML and Stamford routes remain to exit in parallel to the north. The down line of the latter is electrified as far as Helpston and acts as the Slow line for the main route.

At Werrington Junction a secondary route departs east to Spalding and carries a service to that agricultural centre and on over the former GN&GE Joint line to Lincoln and Doncaster. After its authorisation by Parliament the Great Northern Railway worked on this section first because of the ease of construction over the flat countryside, opening the first portion in 1848 and reaching Doncaster via Lincoln in the following year. Services between London and York then ran this way until the opening of the 'Towns Line' through Grantham and Retford cut 20 miles off the journey from 1852.

After a succession of level crossings and the departure of the Stamford line (down) at Helpston, the main line passes through the former station at Tallington. This retains its railway association through the concrete sleeper works (up), which has supplied many of the sleepers for the rail network. No longer is the track made up of bullhead rails sitting in metal 'chairs' on creosoted wooden sleepers. Today good wear and a smooth ride are ensured by continuous welded rails clip-fitted to concrete sleepers. Just before Tallington the old Soke of Peterborough area of Northamptonshire, now part of Cambridgeshire, gives way to agricultural Lincolnshire.

A few former railway buildings still mark the site of the one-time railway junction of Essendine. On both sides the remains of its two branches are also visible, one of the embankments heading east toward Bourne and the other west for Stamford. The Marquis of Exeter contributed to the Stamford line in its indepen-

---

Opening and closing dates
Main line - opened to Retford 15.7.1852 (goods), 1.8.1852 (passengers).
Tallington, Essendine and Little Bytham closed 15.6.1959.
Peterborough Wisbech - opened 1.6.1866 (goods), 1.8.1866 (passengers); closed 2.3.1959.
Peterborough-Spalding - opened 17.10.1848, to Doncaster via Lincoln 4.9.1849.
Essendine-Stamford - opened 1.11.1856, closed 15.6.1959.
Essendine-Bourne - opened 16.6.1860, closed 18.6.1951.
Bourne Saxby - Opened 1.5.1894, closed 2.3.1959.

TALLINGTON: The Great Northern Railway's first big commercial success, the one that finally brought a smile to the faces of the long-suffering shareholders, was securing the movement of South Yorkshire coal to London, and for over 100 years wagonload coal traffic was then to be a familiar sight on the East Coast Main Line, standing in the yards at Doncaster, New England or Ferme Park or on the move as in this photograph taken near Tallington on 10 July 1960. Heading the train is Class '02/2' 2-8-0 No 63939, a representative of a design that originated with the GNR in 1921 and went on to become one of the LNER standard classes. A total of 66 of these heavy goods engines was built.

In the same place but moving about 100 mph faster, the 07.50 Inverness-King's Cross HST, the 'Highland Chieftain', races south on 27 August 1994, Class 43 power car No 43039 leading. *Philip H. Wells/BM*

dent days as some compensation for earlier objections to the routing of the main line through Stamford.

The main line route is climbing now, but the countryside remains agricultural. The area is quite beautiful in an undramatic way, rolling green fields interspersed with wooded areas and picture postcard villages - a very English scene.

Beyond the former Little Bytham station are visible the bridge abutments of a cross-country line that once linked Saxby with the M&GN system and carried many a Midlands summer holidaymaker to his East Coast destination.

The main line is used by services from East Anglia to the North West between Peterborough and Grantham, but it is mainly the province of the trains of InterCity East Coast, whose ECML service is operated by 31 sets of Class 91 locomotives and Mk IV coaches together with nine InterCity 125 diesel-electric High Speed Trains for the non-electrified services to Hull, Harrogate, Aberdeen and Inverness. The InterCity 225 electric trains are made up of the locomotive at the country end, eight or nine coaches and a Driving Van Trailer at the southern, London end. On southbound journeys the trailing locomotive propels with the driver's control exercised by the use of Time Division Multiplex equipment from the DVT.

ESSENDINE: Until its closure from 15 June 1959 Essendine was a rural main-line junction. The 1856 branch from the outer face of the down island platform went to Stamford where the terminus was built in the same style as Burghley House, home of the line's sponsor, the Marquis of Exeter. From the up bay a second branch was opened in 1860, this time to Bourne where the private house used for station purposes had a ghostly reputation! Today some of the Essendine buildings still survive, including the station master's substantial house, preserving a Great Northern touch in a location that elsewhere is a picture of clean, fast track and straightforward overhead equipment. *G. Body*

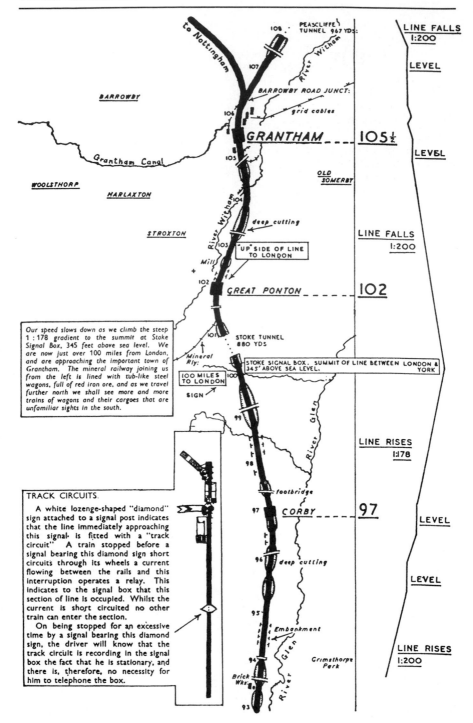

to Nottingham

PEASCLIFFE
TUNNEL 967 YDS:

108

107

River Witham

LINE FALLS
1:200

LEVEL

BARROWBY ROAD JUNCT:

BARROWBY

106

grid cables

GRANTHAM _ _ _ **105½**

105

LEVEL

Grantham Canal

WOOLSTHORP

HARLAXTON

OLD
SOMERBY

104

River Witham

deep cutting

STROXTON

103

"UP" SIDE OF LINE
TO LONDON

LINE FALLS
1:200

Mill

102

GREAT PONTON _ _ _ _ **102**

Our speed slows down as we climb the steep
1 : 178 gradient to the summit at Stoke
Signal Box, 345 feet above sea level. We
are now just over 100 miles from London,
and are approaching the important town of
Grantham. The mineral railway joining us
from the left is lined with tub-like steel
wagons, full of red iron ore, and as we travel
further north we shall see more and more
trains of wagons and their cargoes that are
unfamiliar sights in the south.

101

STOKE TUNNEL
880 YDS

Mineral
Rly:

STOKE SIGNAL BOX. SUMMIT OF LINE BETWEEN LONDON &
345' ABOVE SEA LEVEL.   YORK

100 MILES
TO LONDON

100

SIGN

99

River Glen

LINE RISES
1:178

98

TRACK CIRCUITS.

A white lozenge-shaped "diamond"
sign attached to a signal post indicates
that the line immediately approaching
this signal· is fitted with a "track
circuit" A train stopped before a
signal bearing this diamond sign short
circuits through its wheels a current
flowing between the rails and this
interruption operates a relay. This
indicates to the signal box that this
section of line is occupied. Whilst the
current is short circuited no other
train can enter the section.

On being stopped for an excessive
time by a signal bearing this diamond
sign, the driver will know that the
track circuit is recording in the signal
box the fact that he is stationary, and
there is, therefore, no necessity for
him to telephone the box.

footbridge

97

CORBY _ _ _ _ **97**

LEVEL

96

deep cutting

LEVEL

95

Embankment

River Glen

94

Grimsthorpe
Park

LINE RISES
1:200

Brick
Wks

93

Little Bytham to Grantham

The section of railway line between Helpston and Stoke Tunnel is possibly the most famous in Great Britain. In the up direction nearly 20 miles of falling gra dient have contributed to hundreds of high-speed runs, most notable among them that of *Mallard* in 1938, which produced a world speed record for steam traction. The latest in a long line of outstanding achievements occurred on 2 June 1995 when a new record of 155 mph was established just south of Little Bytham. The train used was a special InterCity 225 set consisting of Class 91 locomotive No 91031 in the rear, five Mk IV coaches and DVT No 82231 at the leading end.

Other milestones in the East Coast Main Line's high-speed history have included:

100 mph by 'A1' Class No 4472 *Flying Scotsman* on 30.11.34

108 mph by 'A3' Class No 2570 *Papyrus* on 5.3.35

112.5 mph by 'A4' Class No 2509 *Silver Link* on 27.9.35

113 mph by 'A4' Class No 2512 *Silver Fox* on 27.8.36

126 mph by 'A4' Class No 4468 *Mallard* on 3.7.38

143.2 mph by prototype HST on 12.6.73

144 mph by 'Tees-Tyne Pullman' HST on 27.9.85

Not all of these took place on Stoke Bank, but an indication of its stature is that it retains the special green flashing signals used for high-speed test runs with the InterCity 225s in the late 1980s.

The down direction climb to pierce the limestone ridge at Stoke Tunnel presents no real challenge to today's powerful motive power. In the process the trains speed through the former station serving Corby Glen village (up), which takes its name from the River Glen and is known for its annual sheep fair dating back to the times of Henry III.

The lonely signal box that once stood before the south portal of Stoke Tunnel has now gone, leaving trains to thunder past the feeder station and into the half-mile bore that marks the highest point on the East Coast Main Line. The four tracks reduce to two for their passage through the tunnel and there is an emergency crossover here.

Milepost 101 north of the tunnel marks the boundary between the

Opening and closing dates
Main line - Corby Glen closed 15.6.1959, Great Ponton 15.9.1958.
Grantham-Nottingham - opened 15.7.1850.
Grantham-Boston - opened to Sleaford 16.6.1857, to Boston 13.4.1859.

Peterborough and Doncaster signalling panels. Unlike the 1947 situation, all sections of the main line are now covered by track circuits with the position of all trains appearing on the distant control panels to facilitate their passage and safety.

The Roman Ermine Street crossed the line here, now in the guise of the B6403 road, and it is still possible to spot (down) the trackbed of the old iron ore branch to Stainby and Sproxton, together with the area occupied by its exchange sidings.

The main line now picks up the valley of the infant River Witham and crosses several deep clefts on its descent to Grantham. This is an important junction for the Nottingham and Skegness lines with a modernised up main platform and down island, but without the renowned loco shed that once provided fresh engines for most of the top main-line services. Through rail services have the advantage of some track realignment, which has reduced the effects of the curves through the complex. Important in times past as a major staging point on the Great North Road, Grantham is dominated by the spire of the 13th-century St Wulfram's church, at 272 feet high one of the tallest in England.

North of Grantham is Nottingham Branch Junction where the double-track route to Nottingham veers off to the west. The Great Northern used this line to attract East Midlands passengers to its King's Cross route, but upset the rival Midland Railway so much that they impounded one of the GN's engines and locked it in an old engine shed at Nottingham.

Left GRANTHAM was an important stopping point for coaches on the old Great North Road and for engine changes on the railway main line in the steam era. Grantham shed (later 34F) stood on the left of the first picture, which was taken from the London end of the complex on 24 May 1980. In it Class 40 No 40117 begins the climb to Stoke summit at the head of nine coaches forming the 08.05 York to King's Cross.

A plethora of overhead catenary and support masts now completely obliterates Grantham station from the same viewpoint, and foliage on the right prevents an exact angle being used. On 7 September 1994 Class 46/7 No 47676 *Northamptonshire* heads south with an Inspection Saloon past a track layout much simplified compared with 14 years earlier. The Aveling-Barford factory on the right has been demolished, emptying the area traditionally occupied by Grantham's heavy industry. *Both BM*

Above right The East Coast Main Line around Barkston and Grantham and down

By courtesy of Sir Nigel Gresley, C.B.E., D.Sc.

ASSOCIATED LOCOMOTIVE EQUIPMENT Lᵀᴰ.
66 VICTORIA ST LONDON S.W.1

Stoke Bank towards Essendine will always be associated with *Mallard*'s epic speed record run during a braking trial on 3 July 1938, remembered in this 1939 advertisement from the makers of the locomotive's blastpipe.

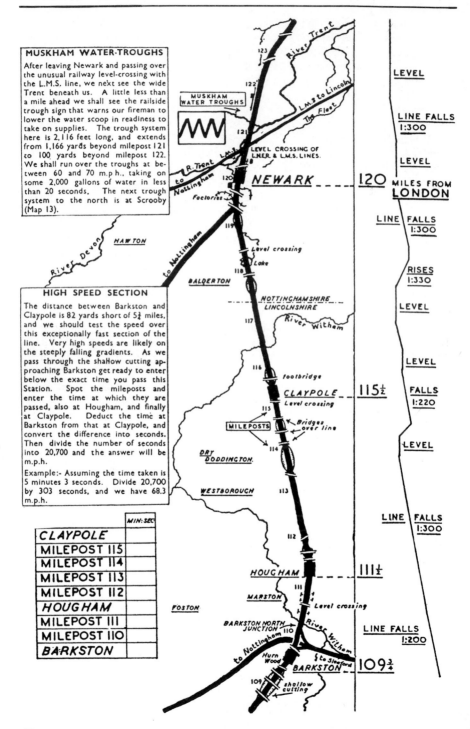

MUSKHAM WATER-TROUGHS

After leaving Newark and passing over the unusual railway level-crossing with the L.M.S. line, we next see the wide Trent beneath us. A little less than a mile ahead we shall see the railside trough sign that warns our fireman to lower the water scoop in readiness to take on supplies. The trough system here is 2,116 feet long, and extends from 1,166 yards beyond milepost 121 to 100 yards beyond milepost 122. We shall run over the troughs at between 60 and 70 m.p h., taking on some 2,000 gallons of water in less than 20 seconds. The next trough system to the north is at Scrooby (Map 13).

HIGH SPEED SECTION

The distance between Barkston and Claypole is 82 yards short of 5¾ miles, and we should test the speed over this exceptionally fast section of the line. Very high speeds are likely on the steeply falling gradients. As we pass through the shallow cutting approaching Barkston get ready to enter below the exact time you pass this Station. Spot the mileposts and enter the time at which they are passed, also at Hougham, and finally at Claypole. Deduct the time at Barkston from that at Claypole, and convert the difference into seconds. Then divide the number of seconds into 20,700 and the answer will be m.p.h.

Example:- Assuming the time taken is 5 minutes 3 seconds. Divide 20,700 by 303 seconds, and we have 68.3 m.p.h.

	MIN:SEC
CLAYPOLE	
MILEPOST 115	
MILEPOST 114	
MILEPOST 113	
MILEPOST 112	
HOUGHAM	
MILEPOST 111	
MILEPOST 110	
BARKSTON	

MUSKHAM WATER TROUGHS

LEVEL CROSSING OF L.N.E.R. & L.M.S. LINES.

NEWARK — 120 MILES FROM LONDON

HAWTON

BALDERTON

Level crossing

Lake

NOTTINGHAMSHIRE
LINCOLNSHIRE

River Witham

footbridge

CLAYPOLE — 115½
Level crossing

MILEPOSTS — Bridges over line

DRY DODDINGTON

WESTBOROUGH

HOUGHAM — 111¼

MARSTON

FOSTON

Level crossing

BARKSTON NORTH JUNCTION 110

Hurn Wood

BARKSTON — 109¾

shallow cutting

LEVEL

LINE FALLS 1:300

LEVEL

LINE FALLS 1:300

RISES 1:330

LEVEL

LEVEL

FALLS 1:220

LEVEL

LINE FALLS 1:300

LINE FALLS 1:200

Barkston to Newark

Emerging from Peascliffe Tunnel the East Coast Main line now comes to Barkston where the largely double-track route to Sleaford, Boston and Skegness departs eastwards. From this line at Honington there used to be a branch carrying a Grantham to Lincoln service, but this ended in 1965. Barkston does retain its 1875 connection from Allington Junction on the Grantham-Nottingham line, but it no longer carries the heavily-loaded trains of holidaymakers from the Manchester area and the East Midlands to the resorts of Skegness, Mablethorpe and Sutton-on-Sea. On the up side of the line there are traces of the former spur between Barkston East and North junctions which was used by *Mallard* to run round its down train before the 1938 record-breaking run.

The high ground is now left behind and the scenery changes to an area of flat, fertile farmland. The four-track profile of the main line has also changed to one of two tracks plus passing loops. One such loop is located at the site of the former Claypole station where the one-time signal box survives (down) to control a group of crossings and where there is also an emergency crossover.

Just beyond Claypole the River Witham passes beneath the railway, now heading east for Lincoln and the Wash and forming part of the Lincolnshire/Nottinghamshire boundary as it does so. Just in Notts the village of Balderton (down) has associations with Lady Godiva and with a performer of a different kind, Sir Donald Wolfit.

Newark is preceded by the site (down) of the former South Junction from which the Great Northern had a line penetrating south to Nottingham and Leicester and eventually to Market Harborough. The town of Newark itself was established because of its prime and strategic location at the meeting of the Fosse Way, the Great North Road and the River Trent. King John died in the castle visible above the town on the down side and Newark, with its Royalist garrison, was besieged three times in the course of the Civil War, the final Parliamentary victory resulting in the demolition of the castle.

Newark's main railway importance is as the meeting point of two rail routes, that of the East Coast Main Line running north-south and of the Nottingham to Lincoln line running east-west. The latter was one of the projects of George Hudson, the so-called 'Railway King', and was built in a great hurry in order to give his Midland lines a connection to Lincoln before the Great Northern could get there.

The two rail routes cross on the level north of the ECML's Newark Northgate

Opening and closing dates
Main line - Barkston closed 16.3.1955, Hougham 16.9.1957, Claypole 16.9.1957.
Grantham/Honington-Lincoln - Opened 15.4.1867, closed 1.11.1965.
Bottesford-Newark - opened 1.7.1878, closed 7.12.1953.
Nottingham-Lincoln - opened 3.8.1846.

NEWARK is an historic market town on the River Trent and is served by two railway routes, that of the East Coast Main Line and the lesser, but still important, ex-Midland Railway line from Nottingham to Lincoln. Newark's two separate stations are known, respectively, as Northgate and Castle, the 'past' view here giving a good impression of Northgate in Great Northern days. The sheer volume of signs and posters is amazing, but those were the days when each platform had its Ladies, Gents and General waiting rooms, not to mention Left Luggage, Refreshment Room, Telegraph Office and other such places that had to be labelled.

With the Potts station clock and a little of the old down-side canopy still in place, modern Newark is a much simpler, better-lit station and is also an hour 'nearer' to King's Cross! The photograph taken there on 8 September 1994 shows the 06.00 Edinburgh to King's Cross service sweeping through the station with the driver in Mk IV DVT No 82228 and Class 91 No 91011 *Terence Cuneo* pushing from the rear. *Lens of Sutton/BM*

station, this forming the sole surviving example of a flat crossing along the course of the main line. With the closure of the Grantham-Lincoln branch, main-line traffic for the latter point was routed via Newark and a new connection put in between the two routes to facilitate this. Nowadays King's Cross-Lincoln passengers can do the journey in under 2 hours compared with 3 or more under LNER timings.

BARKSTON: Passing Barkston South Junction at speed on 6 August 1994, Mk IV DVT No 82210 leads the 08.00 Glasgow Central-King's Cross express with a Class 91, out of sight, providing traction from the rear in accordance with the standard pattern of ECML working. Barkston used to have its own station at this point until it lost its trains from 16 March 1955, but the location is better remembered as the place at which *Mallard* turned its train before embarking upon the run that produced the 126 mph world record for steam traction. After arriving from London the down train ran from Barkston South Junction to Barkston East, where the Sleaford/Boston line is joined by that from Allington Junction on the Nottingham branch, and then reversed back to the main line over the now-abandoned spur to Barkston North. *Ken Brunt*

NEWARK: The East Coast Main Line used to have 'flat' crossings at Newark, Retford and Darlington, but only that at Newark survives. Such a crossing really represents no greater complication than a junction would; indeed, the section blocked by the crossing train will tend to clear more quickly, although it still has a limiting effect on the paths available on the busy main line. This scene on 23 March 1991 shows the 16.20 Leeds-King's Cross service, which has passed over the bridge across the River Trent and then the Nottingham-Lincoln line and is heading for Newark station. A Mk IV DVT leads and Class 91 No 91011 propels. This vantage point gives a good view of the Trent bridge. *BM*

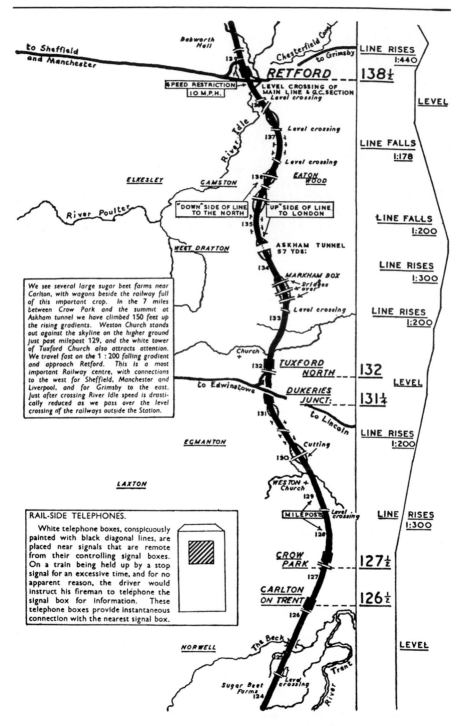

Newark to Retford

Leaving Newark the main line passes beneath the A46 trunk road, crosses the Lincoln line, then bridges the River Trent. Locks on the latter and the Newark sugar beet factory can be seen on the down side preceding another stretch of flat farmland dominated by the Trent and the A1 successor to the Great North Road (up). South Muskham and its church (down) were another Civil War hotspot.

On via the site of Carlton-on-Trent station, still marked by a level crossing, an up passenger loop and an emergency crossover, the main line comes to what is left of the Tuxford railway conurbation, the approaches (up) offering a view of the impressive Lincoln cathedral in the distance. Dating from 1311 and standing high on a hill overlooking the city, the cathedral is one of the highest buildings in the world and one of exceptional beauty.

Along the main line an overbridge, now singled, carries the remains of the grandly titled Lancashire, Derbyshire & East Coast Railway, which justified its name by linking the system at Chesterfield with that at Lincoln. After passenger closure in 1955 part of the route was retained as a freight line to serve High Marnham power station, now providing Mainline Freight with a 250,000-ton coal supply contract.

To the east High Marnham power station is visible along with its neighbour Cottam and, further away, West Burton. These three were opened in 1962, 1970 and 1968 respectively to provide a massive contribution to the National Grid, the later stations each having four 500-megawatt turbo-generators. Away to the west, north of Sherwood Forest, is Bevercotes Colliery.

The point at which the LD&EC route crossed the main line was the site of Dukeries Junction, a station with high-level and low-level platforms to serve both routes. Another link between the two ran from the Chesterfield-Lincoln line down to Tuxford North, located a little along the ECML and where the old goods yard is still apparent (down).

The tiny Askham Tunnel now takes the main line through a small rise in the terrain and helps it forward to a crossing of the River Idle and entry into Retford. Rather grand up-side buildings testify to the station's Great Northern Railway heritage, but in many other ways Retford has changed considerably. Notable among these changes is the elimination of the old flat crossing south of the station where the main line was intersected by that of the former Great Central Railway's east-west corridor from Sheffield to Cleethorpes. The penal speed restrictions resulting

---

Opening and closing dates
Main line - Lincoln-Retford-Doncaster opened 4.9.1849. Carlton-on-Trent closed 2.3.1953, Crow Park 6.10.1958, Dukeries Junction 7.3.1950, Tuxford North 4.7.1955.
Chesterfield-Lincoln - opened 8.3.1897, closed 19.9.1955.
Retford-Sheffield-Gainsborough - opened 16.7.1849.

TUXFORD: The road ahead is clear for a southbound express passing Tuxford North station on 24 May 1959 and hauled by Doncaster (36A)-allocated Gresley 'A3' Class 'Pacific' No 60066 *Merry Hampton*. Until four years earlier Tuxford had also boasted a station on the ex-LD&EC line from Chesterfield Market Place to Lincoln. Surviving after passenger closure to serve High Marnham power station, this crossed the main line ahead of *Merry Hampton* at Dukeries Junction where the two-level station closed in 1950. In the right foreground of this picture is an excellent example of the then modern semaphore signal with concrete posts. The 'on' arm controls access to the spur leading round to Tuxford Central.

Passing the site of the old Tuxford North station on 7 September 1994, the DVT-led 08.00 Glasgow Central-King's Cross InterCity 225 service has the usual Class 91 rear-end power, in this case provided by No 91002 *Durham Cathedral*. Although the station and surrounding buildings have gone, the chimneys of the house in the top right-hand corner are still apparent behind the trees. *Both BM*

from the flat crossing were removed by constructing a dive-under for the cross-country line, which also had its platforms moved to give better interchange between the two routes.

The line to Sheffield featured in another Great Northern attempt to abstract traffic from other routes to its own. This was the way the GN got to Sheffield and later attacked the Euston route's monopoly of the Manchester business, the small and impoverished Manchester, Sheffield & Lincolnshire Railway, as the Great Central then was, getting rather caught in the middle of the resulting conflict.

Leaving Retford, with the single-line connection between the two routes visible on the down side, the main line crosses the Chesterfield Canal, linking Worksop with the River Trent and another product of the coal business, and continues its journey northwards.

Right **The rather grand up-side buildings at Retford carry this unusual plaque.** *G. Body*

Below **RETFORD: In the original InterCity blue/grey livery, the King's Cross-bound 'Flying Scotsman' HST approaches Retford on 6 September 1980. The Class 254 sets built for the East Coast Main Line consisted of two 1st Class and six Standard Class vehicles, as in this case where set No 254023 is headed by power car No 43101.** *BM*

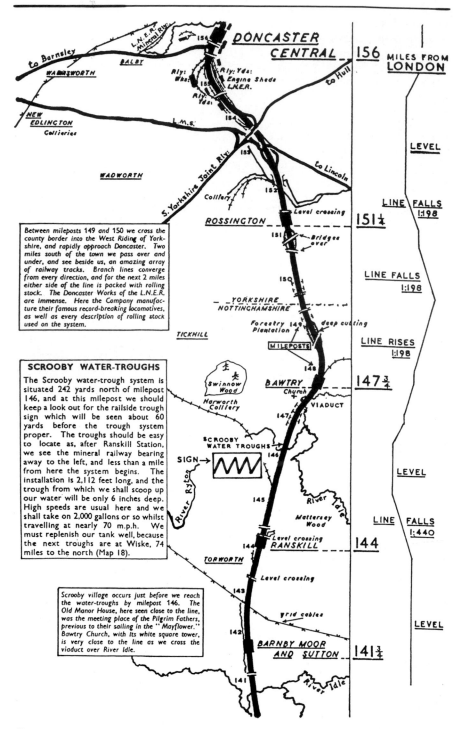

Between mileposts 149 and 150 we cross the county border into the West Riding of Yorkshire, and rapidly approach Doncaster. Two miles south of the town we pass over and under, and see beside us, an amazing array of railway tracks. Branch lines converge from every direction, and for the next 2 miles either side of the line is packed with rolling stock. The Doncaster Works of the L.N.E.R. are immense. Here the Company manufacture their famous record-breaking locomotives, as well as every description of rolling stock used on the system.

SCROOBY WATER-TROUGHS

The Scrooby water-trough system is situated 242 yards north of milepost 146, and at this milepost we should keep a look out for the railside trough sign which will be seen about 60 yards before the trough system proper. The troughs should be easy to locate as, after Ranskill Station, we see the mineral railway bearing away to the left, and less than a mile from here the system begins. The installation is 2,112 feet long, and the trough from which we shall scoop up our water will be only 6 inches deep. High speeds are usual here and we shall take on 2,000 gallons or so whilst travelling at nearly 70 m.p.h. We must replenish our tank well, because the next troughs are at Wiske, 74 miles to the north (Map 18).

Scrooby village occurs just before we reach the water-troughs by milepost 146. The Old Manor House, here seen close to the line, was the meeting place of the Pilgrim Fathers, previous to their sailing in the "Mayflower." Bawtry Church, with its white square tower, is very close to the line as we cross the viaduct over River Idle.

Barnby Moor to Doncaster

Beyond the sites of the former stations at Barnby Moor & Sutton and Ranskill the line again crosses the River Idle near Scrooby village and the location of the steam era water troughs. The original founder of the Pilgrim Fathers was baptised at St Wilfred's church (down) at Scrooby in 1566 and nearby Austerfield (up) is also similarly connected with the early history of the United States. By the lineside along this stretch of the East Coast Main Line the LNER erected signs marking '250 miles to Edinburgh' near milepost 143 and then, nearer Doncaster, 'London 150'. Both can still be seen today.

At Bawtry, once intended as the junction for the route to Sheffield, an overgrown trackbed (up) marks the course of the goods line that used to run to Misson. Along the main line there were a number of small depots used exclusively for goods traffic, but few traces remain of these. After crossing into South Yorkshire the first township is Rossington (down) followed by the colliery, which is its principal employer. The rail connection to the colliery remains in use, the coal activity contrasting with the Potteric Carr Nature Reserve opposite.

The line now crosses an area of marshy ground and passes under the M18 to come to the first set of Doncaster junctions where four routes from the south made their complicated connections, now much simplified. The Decoy yard area that follows no longer handles the thousands of small coal wagons that had been tripped in from the collieries of the South Yorkshire coalfield and were to be fed out again along the two main routes to the south. Doncaster locomotive depot and the activities of the civil engineer now occupy the siding area on the up side of the line, with the old airport and the famous Doncaster racecourse further east still. The original Great Northern Railway entrepreneurs got some of the first returns on the huge outlay involved in building the main line by running specials for racegoers at Doncaster.

On the opposite side of the line is the modernised Belmont yard, created in a major remodelling of the whole Doncaster area and now handling its residual freight business, the coal, oil and other bulk commodities that pass in trainload or large consignment quantities. It is followed (down) by the junction with the Sheffield line, which brings local and InterCity cross-country services to connect

---

Opening and closing dates
Main line - Barnby Moor & Sutton closed 7.11.1949, Ranskill 6.10.1958, Scrooby 14.9.1931, Bawtry and Rossington 6.10.1958.
Doncaster-Sheffield - opened to Swinton 10.11.1849 (Swinton- Sheffield 1.7.1840).
Doncaster-Gainsborough - opened 1.7.1867 (goods), 15.7.1867 (passengers).
Dinnington-Kirk Sandall - opened 1.1.1909 (goods), 1.10.1910 (passengers); closed 2.12.1929.
Dearne Valley Line - opened 1.1.1909 (goods), 3.6.1912 (passengers); closed 10.9.1951.

with Doncaster's main-line expresses, the trains to and from the West Riding and those on the Lincoln, Cleethorpes and Humberside lines.

The Doncaster operational activity, together with that of the whole route from Stoke Tunnel to the beginning of the Selby Diversion, is controlled from the signalling panel in the old goods yard (up) preceding the station. The latter consists of two island platforms with bays, with the main lines running between. The town centre and its modern shopping complex lies nearby to the east, while opposite stands the famous Doncaster 'Plant' where so many of the LNER's locomotives and rolling stock were designed and built. Although no longer fulfilling this function the railway connection is maintained by the repair and maintenance work of ABB Support Systems.

A measure of the changes since the *Mile by Mile* booklet was produced is that the steam services of the past covered the journey from London to Doncaster, with a stop at Peterborough, in 174 minutes. Today such a journey will take only 92 minutes for the 156 miles, just over 100 mph!

DONCASTER: Spotters to the left of us, spotters to the right of us. . . On a typical summer Saturday at Doncaster in the 1950s, holding centre stage in the photograph is Class 'B16/3' 4-6-0 No 61464 coasting into the station on 23 May 1959 with an express for Hull. Stock to the right includes a double-cylinder gas tank, while 'perishable' vans are being shunted past the goods depot, itself full of box vans.

With a Class 142 'Pacer' in the Doncaster bay platform forming a local service to Sheffield, the centrepiece of the more recent view is an InterCity Cross Country HST. The service is the 10.43 Bristol Temple Meads to York with Class 43 power car No 43029 leading. Quite a lot has changed in 15 years, including the bridge from which the previous photographs were taken. Doncaster's up platform has been lengthened using space vacated by access lines to the old goods depot and much of the down-side trackwork has gone, matching the reduction in activity in the former Works. There are no spotters to be seen and the church is sandwiched between a tower block and the Doncaster panel building. *Both BM*

Below **This is the London end of Doncaster station in Great Northern days, showing just how extensive are the changes time has wrought. Who now remembers Shakespeare signal box, the old up-side end-dock or the sidings in front of 'The Plant' being so full? Only the footbridge access to the Works seems to have survived without significant alteration. The bridge from which the photograph was taken was the scene of a 1951 derailment accident in which 14 people were killed.** *Lens of Sutton*

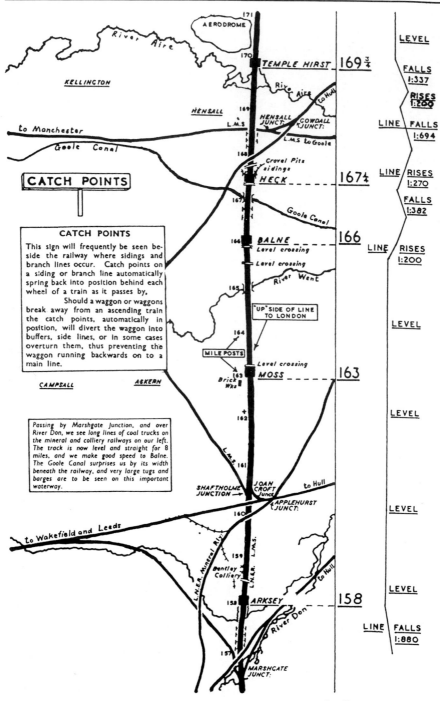

CATCH POINTS

CATCH POINTS

This sign will frequently be seen beside the railway where sidings and branch lines occur. Catch points on a siding or branch line automatically spring back into position behind each wheel of a train as it passes by,

     Should a waggon or waggons break away from an ascending train the catch points, automatically in position, will divert the waggon into buffers, side lines, or in some cases overturn them, thus preventing the waggon running backwards on to a main line.

Passing by Marshgate Junction, and over River Don, we see long lines of coal trucks on the mineral and colliery railways on our left. The track is now level and straight for 8 miles, and we make good speed to Balne. The Goole Canal surprises us by its width beneath the railway, and very large tugs and barges are to be seen on this important waterway.

See Errata

Doncaster to Temple Hirst

The radio mast seen on leaving Doncaster station (down) is a reminder of the vast advances in railway telecommunications since the days of the LNER. Back in 1947 relatively little use was made of non-railway telephone lines and many messages were conveyed either over local circuits - which could theoretically be linked, but in practice made effective conversation nearly impossible - or by the single needle telegraph instrument. Every station of size had a telegraph office for handling internal and public messages, but there was just nothing to compare with today's systems, which range from the use of fibre-optic cables carrying multiple message fragments to complex interlinked computer systems.

At Marshgate Junction, Doncaster, the line passes over the River Don and its canalised companion, and the routes to Wakefield and Hull depart on either side. Overhead is the Avoiding Line, which links the Sheffield and Humberside routes and was built to keep freight traffic out of the busy Doncaster station complex. It still fulfils this function.

Although the East Coast Main Line label refers primarily to the route from King's Cross to Newcastle and its extension north to Edinburgh to serve the east coast of Scotland, the services to and from the West Riding have always been an important adjunct. The original LNER streamlined services introduced between King's Cross and Newcastle and Edinburgh were soon followed by the 'West Riding Limited' designed to cater for Leeds and Bradford passengers and the woollen industry they frequently represented. Today's InterCity 225 services cover the 186 miles to Leeds in slightly over 2 hours, around 40 minutes better than even the streamlined 'Pacific' locomotives *Golden Fleece* and *Golden Shuttle* could manage.

Beyond the closed Arksey station there is a link with another avoiding line and a junction with a surviving single line to Knottingley. This is Shaftholme Junction, an historic spot once marking the northern extremity of the Great Northern Railway's territory. Its first trains to York, from 8 August 1850, reached there via Knottingley and Burton Salmon over the lines of the Lancashire & Yorkshire and York & North Midland companies. Later the more direct route to York via Selby

---

Opening and closing dates

Main line - Shaftholme Junction to Chaloner Whin Junction opened 2.1.1871. Arksey closed 5.8.1952, Moss 8.6.1953, Balne and Heck 15.9.1958, Temple Hirst 6.3.1961.

Doncaster-Knottingley - Knottingley-Stockbridge opened 6.6.1848, to Doncaster 7.9.1848; closed 27.9.1948.

Doncaster Avoiding Line - opened 25.7.1910.

Doncaster-Hull - opened to Thorne 1.7.1856, to Hull 2.8.1869.

Doncaster-Grimsby - opened to Thorne 11.12.1855 (goods), 1.7.1856 (passengers), to Keadby 10.9.1859, to Barnetby 1.5.1866 (goods), 1.10.1856 (passengers).

Doncaster-Wakefield - opened 1.2.1866.

MARSHGATE JUNCTION, just north of Doncaster station, is where the East Coast Main Line parts company with the lines to Hull and Wakefield. Here, on 31 August 1954, Robinson Class 'J11' 0-6-0 No 64404 trundles into Doncaster with a Sheffield-bound freight working. The first examples of the 'J11' Class were built as far back as 1901 by the Great Central Railway. They were a familiar sight in the Doncaster area because of its extensive GCR connections.

Overhead wires for Doncaster's public transport have gone from the bridge, but the railway below now has them in profusion. On 28 August 1994 Class 37/7 No 37886 passes beneath the same bridge with southbound steel wagons. Behind this the railway crosses the River Don from which Doncaster takes its name. *Both BM*

was opened in 1871 by the North Eastern Railway, the boundary at Shaftholme Junction subsequently marking the meeting point of the LNER's Southern and Northern Divisions.

This is a straight, level section of the main line studded with level crossings and passing through fertile arable land. Thorpe Marsh power station (up) marks the beginning of a whole landscape of such installations but, out of sight, is the compensation of a large nature reserve created in the process of building the generating plant.

After the River Went the main line crosses first over the Airc & Calder Navigation, then under the M62 and finally over the Knottingley-Goole line, which still carries a sparse passenger train service. There are also traces of the old Hull & Barnsley Railway, built to carry coal to the Humber but a latecomer on the railway scene and an early departure from it.

Right **A page from an LNER pamphlet for the streamlined 'West Riding Limited'.**

Below **DONCASTER WORKS: We shouldn't leave Doncaster without a brief visit to the famous 'Plant'. Inside the Works on 23 May 1959 the scene appears one of great confusion with locomotives lifted off their leading wheels and others with their driving gear in apparently meaningless disarray. But this was all part of the rich panoply of 'shopping programmes' for heavy locomotive repairs, with the 'victims' in this case being BR Standard '7MT' Class 'Pacific' No 70039 *Sir Christopher Wren*, Class 'A3' 'Pacifics' Nos 60107 *Royal Lancer* and 60064 *Tagalie*, and Class 'A2' 'Pacific' No 60534 *Irish Elegance*.** *DM*

"WEST RIDING LIMITED"

Since their inception the L.N.E.R streamline train services between London and Newcastle ("The Silver Jubilee") and London and Edinburgh ("The Coronation") have won their place in the list of the world's most famous trains. With every confidence in the public patronage of further services of this character, combining high speed with high standard of comfort and punctuality, the London & North Eastern Railway Company introduced the "West Riding Limited" between London, Leeds and Bradford.

The times of departure and arrival are :—

Bradford (Exchange)	dep.	11.10 a.m.
Leeds (Central)	dep.	11.31 a.m.
London (King's Cross)	arr.	2.15 p.m.
London (King's Cross)	dep.	7.10 p.m.
Leeds (Central)	arr.	9.53 p.m.
Bradford (Exchange)	arr.	10.15 p.m.

(See pages 10 and 11 for Mileage Tables.)

The "West Riding Limited" is intended for the use of passengers to and from London only.

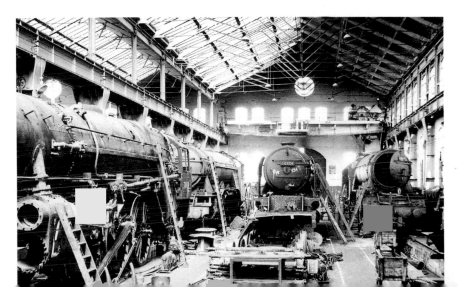

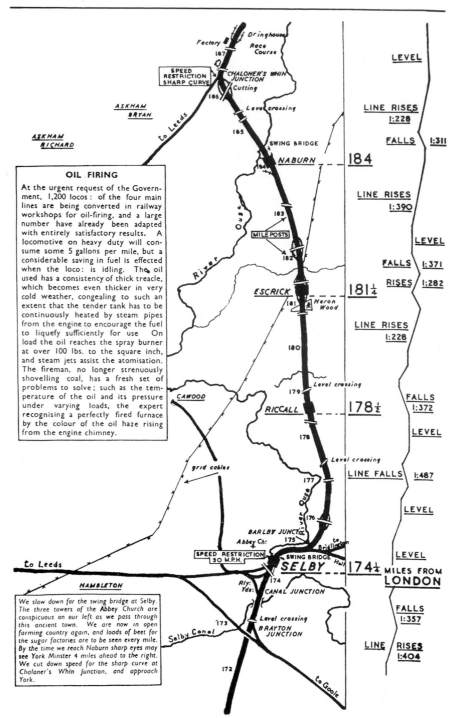

OIL FIRING

At the urgent request of the Government, 1,200 locos : of the four main lines are being converted in railway workshops for oil-firing, and a large number have already been adapted with entirely satisfactory results. A locomotive on heavy duty will consume some 5 gallons per mile, but a considerable saving in fuel is effected when the loco: is idling. The oil used has a consistency of thick treacle, which becomes even thicker in very cold weather, congealing to such an extent that the tender tank has to be continuously heated by steam pipes from the engine to encourage the fuel to liquefy sufficiently for use   On load the oil reaches the spray burner at over 100 lbs. to the square inch, and steam jets assist the atomisation. The fireman, no longer strenuously shovelling coal, has a fresh set of problems to solve ; such as the temperature of the oil and its pressure under varying loads, the expert recognising a perfectly fired furnace by the colour of the oil haze rising from the engine chimney.

We slow down for the swing bridge at Selby. The three towers of the Abbey Church are conspicuous on our left as we pass through this ancient town. We are now in open farming country again, and loads of beet for the sugar factories are to be seen every mile. By the time we reach Naburn sharp eyes may see York Minster 4 miles ahead to the right. We cut down speed for the sharp curve at Chaloner's Whin Junction, and approach York.

LEVEL

LINE RISES 1:228

FALLS 1:311

184

LINE RISES 1:390

LEVEL

FALLS 1:371

RISES 1:282

181¼

LINE RISES 1:228

FALLS 1:372

178½

LEVEL

LINE FALLS 1:487

LEVEL

LEVEL

174¼ MILES FROM LONDON

FALLS 1:357

LINE RISES 1:404

Temple Hirst to Chaloner Whin

The biggest changes on the East Coast Main Line in recent years have been its electrification and the 1983 opening of the Selby Diversion. Before the latter, main-line expresses had reached York over the North Eastern Railway's 1871 'cut-off', which had linked Doncaster and Selby and then used an earlier route to cross the River Ouse before continuing north to Chaloner Whin Junction and York. There were speed restrictions over the swing bridge at Selby and again at Chaloner Whin.

North of Selby and the river lay vast, untapped reserves of good clean coal in a thick seam. To exploit this meant either leaving a wide corridor through which the main line could pass free of the risk of subsidence, or imposing severe speed restrictions in the interests of safety. Neither course was acceptable to the railway and coal industries.

Accordingly the decision was taken to divert the main line around the west side of the potential mining area. Under the direction of the railway civil engineer, the contractors, Monk & Co, set about the task of building Britain's first stretch of double-track main line since the Great Central's extension to London at the turn of the century. The total length of the new line, which runs from Temple Hirst Junction to Colton Junction, is 23 km and its construction entailed 2.5 million tonnes of rock fill and common fill, 345,000 tonnes of ballast and 23 road, river and foot bridges.

The northern section from Hambleton Junction on the Leeds-Selby line to Colton Junction on the Leeds-York line was opened on 16 May 1983 and the southern one down to Temple Hirst Junction on 3 October of that year. The track and junctions were designed for full 125 mph running, although lower speeds applied until the track bedded down. The Temple Hirst-Selby section of the old line was retained as a branch, albeit now with a rather sparse Doncaster-Selby train service.

Approaching Temple Hirst involves crossing the River Went, the Aire & Calder Navigation and the M62. Then, before passing over the River Aire, Eggborough 2,000-megawatt power station is visible along the Wakefield line (down) while in the other direction is the mighty 4,000-megawatt Drax complex. A little further north along the new main line the Ferrybridge stations appear in the distance (down) just before we pass over the Selby Canal. West of the Hambleton junctions

---

Opening and closing dates
Main line - Shaftholme Junction to Chaloner Whin Junction opened 2.1.1871; closed north of Selby 24.9.1983. Selby Diversion northern section opened 16.5.1983, southern 3.10.1983.
Leeds-Selby - opened 22.9.1834.
Leeds-York - original route via Gascoigne Wood 19.5.1839, via Methley curve 27.7.1840; opened Church Fenton-Micklefield 1.4.1869.

SELBY: The 'past' picture typifies the East Coast Main Line as it used to be. The southbound 'Talisman' from Edinburgh Waverley to King's Cross on 22 May 1959 is recovering from the 25 mph speed restriction through Selby and pulling away round the curve under clear signals. The locomotive is Class 'A2' 'Pacific' No 60539 *Bronzino* and all around it is the paraphernalia of a mechanically worked, steam-powered railway.

Departing south from Selby on 1 September 1994, West Yorkshire PTE Class 158/9 No 158909 forms the 15.53 train from Selby to Manchester Victoria. The road bridge and lineside hut survive, but very little else! *Both BM*

with the Leeds-Selby-Hull line is Gascoigne Wood where the Selby coal comes to the surface for rail loading; east is the Wistow mine.

Nearing Colton Junction the main line bridges the River Wharfe and is then joined by the connection from the Leeds line. The ECML connection to the Leeds line is then at Colton North Junction with four tracks from there on to York. On the way the old junction at Chaloner Whin is just discernible (up) as is the site (up) of the former marshalling yard at Dringhouses.

Doncaster to York can now take as little as 21 minutes; it used to take twice that or, if you called at all nine intermediate stations, well over an hour. The countryside *en route* may be flat but traversing it is exciting.

Right The Big Switch - a 1983 booklet giving alterations to train services during the change-over from the original main line to the new Selby Coalfield Diversion route.

Below By comparison with the 1959 situation pictured opposite, on the new diversion line what curves there are do not significantly inhibit speed and in this scene, captured on 1 September 1994, the 11.00 King's Cross-Glasgow Central InterCity 225 service is not planning to slow for anything except its scheduled York stop. Class 91 No 91026 is at the front end. *BM*

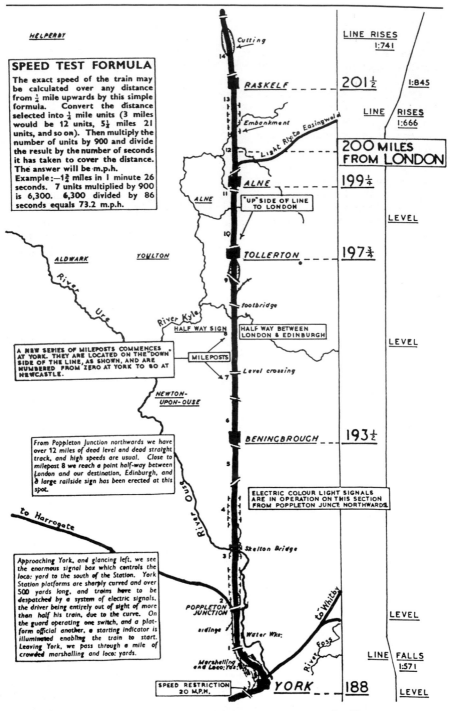

HELPERBY

Cutting

LINE RISES
1:741

RASKELF --- $201\frac{1}{2}$ 1:845

Embankment

LINE / RISES
1:666

Light Rly to Easingwold

200 MILES
FROM LONDON

ALNE --- $199\frac{1}{4}$

ALNE

"UP" SIDE OF LINE
TO LONDON

LEVEL

SPEED TEST FORMULA

The exact speed of the train may be calculated over any distance from $\frac{1}{4}$ mile upwards by this simple formula. Convert the distance selected into $\frac{1}{4}$ mile units (3 miles would be 12 units, $5\frac{1}{4}$ miles 21 units, and so on). Then multiply the number of units by 900 and divide the result by the number of seconds it has taken to cover the distance. The answer will be m.p.h.
Example:—$1\frac{3}{4}$ miles in 1 minute 26 seconds. 7 units multiplied by 900 is 6,300. 6,300 divided by 86 seconds equals 73.2 m.p.h.

ALDWARK   YOULTON

River Ure

TOLLERTON --- $197\frac{3}{4}$

footbridge

River Kyle

HALF WAY SIGN

HALF WAY BETWEEN
LONDON & EDINBURGH

LEVEL

MILEPOSTS

Level crossing

A NEW SERIES OF MILEPOSTS COMMENCES AT YORK. THEY ARE LOCATED ON THE "DOWN" SIDE OF THE LINE, AS SHOWN, AND ARE NUMBERED FROM ZERO AT YORK TO 80 AT NEWCASTLE.

NEWTON-
UPON-OUSE

From Poppleton Junction northwards we have over 12 miles of dead level and dead straight track, and high speeds are usual. Close to milepost 8 we reach a point half-way between London and our destination, Edinburgh, and a large railside sign has been erected at this spot.

BENINGBROUGH --- $193\frac{1}{2}$

River Ouse

ELECTRIC COLOUR LIGHT SIGNALS ARE IN OPERATION ON THIS SECTION FROM POPPLETON JUNCE NORTHWARDS.

to Harrogate

Skelton Bridge

Approaching York, and glancing left, we see the enormous signal box which controls the loco: yard to the south of the Station. York Station platforms are sharply curved and over 500 yards long, and trains have to be despatched by a system of electric signals, the driver being entirely out of sight of more than half his train, due to the curve. On the guard operating one switch, and a platform official another, a starting indicator is illuminated enabling the train to start. Leaving York, we pass through a mile of crowded marshalling and loco: yards.

POPPLETON
JUNCTION

sidings

to Whitby

Water Wks:

LEVEL

River Foss

Marshalling
and Loco: Yds:

LINE / FALLS
1:571

SPEED RESTRICTION
20 M.P.H.

YORK --- 188

LEVEL

See Errata

York to Raskelf

It is fitting that York, an historic city with a great railway tradition, should be the headquarters of the administration of the East Coast Main Line, both the InterCity East Coast trains and the Railtrack ECML infrastructure. The city was the target of the original London & York railway scheme and the home of George Hudson, the so-called 'Railway King' whose unconventional enterprise brought many a line into existence before his eventual downfall. His first line gave York an outlet to the south from 1839 and two years later the Great North of England Railway opened its route northwards through the Vale of York to Darlington.

Today the rail layout at York is much simplified with the loss of the carriage and wagon building activity and of the great locomotive depot south of the station. The latter has been remodelled, its track layout simplified and one platform abandoned, but it remains an imposing and efficient rail interchange point. All operations are controlled from the ultra-modern Electronic Integrated Control Centre.

The present York through station replaced an earlier terminus built in 1841 and reached via an archway in the city walls. The 1853 hotel there was later used as railway offices and the yard for York's first railway museum, but an office block, Hudson House, now occupies the main train shed area.

Today's station was completed in 1877; based on an original design by Thomas Prosser, it was completed by William Peachey. The main feature, four great, curving spans supported on Corinthian columns, remains impressive to this day. The frontage area houses the modern travel centre and leads to the main concourse where there is a North Eastern Railway system map depicted in tiles on one of the walls. Other items of special interest include the footbridge clock and former signal box, an old NER signal, spandrels decorated with the NER monogram and coat of arms, the old tea rooms and the adjoining station hotel. Nearby the 1906 headquarters offices, the old station area and the NER war memorial are worth seeing, as are the many non-railway attractions of this fine old city. York Minster, the city walls and its museums are especially rewarding.

At the north end of York station the Scarborough line departs from up side bay platforms and the National Railway Museum, housing the National Collection and successor to the one-time York and Clapham museums, occupies a former railway goods site in Leeman Road (down). The exhibits in the museum are many and varied, ranging from historic locomotives and rolling-stock to such things as station signs, restaurant cutlery and hundreds of smaller items.

Beyond it the avoiding line around the west side of the York complex rejoins just

---

Opening and closing dates
Main line - York-Darlington opened 4.1.1841 (goods), 30.3.1841 (passengers).
   Beningbrough closed 15.9.1958, Tollerton 1.11.1965, Alne and Raskelf 5.5.1958.
York-Scarborough - opened 7.7.1845.
York-Harrogate - opened to Knaresborough 30.10.1848, throughout 1.10.1851.

YORK: The 1959 view of York shows the complex of station, hotel and former NER head-quarters behind the train, and the loco depot straight ahead. The original station inside the city walls and the old museum site are off-picture to the right, while the avoiding line to the left leads to Holgate Sidings, the Carriage & Wagon Works and adjacent yards, and on to Klondyke Sidings and York Yard North signal box. Through the middle of this scene double-chimney 'A3' 'Pacific' No 60050 *Persimmon* heads south with a Newcastle-King's Cross express on 22 May.

On 1 September 1994 we see the final form of the York rationalisation. Class 158/9 No 158905 approaches its destination with the 10.14 from Hebden Bridge, a service that but for industrial action on that day would have started from Blackpool North. *Both BM*

beyond York Yard North, the yard itself now being used mainly for permanent way and other civil engineering activity. Then comes the sugar beet factory (down) and Skelton Junction at which the route to Leeds via Harrogate departs (down).

After crossing the Ouse at Skelton Bridge the main line heads north, past Beningbrough station with its lineside restaurant complex based on restored coaches, and forward to the halfway point between London and Edinburgh, duly signed to that effect along with the 'Edinburgh 200' location that precedes it.

The 'London 200' sign appears just beyond the site of Alne station, once junction for the Easingwold Light Railway and marking the end of the level section from York. This straight, easy stretch has also featured in speed records including the run on 2 June 1995. Beyond the railway, on the higher slopes of the Hambleton Hills to the east is a white horse image carved on a hillside site of 2 acres in 1857.

Right YORK: There is much of historic railway interest here, including in the station the famous clock, which stands above the footbridge between the main platforms in front of the former signal box and surrounded by elaborate decorative ironwork. *BM*

Below Under one of the four great roof spans of York station Class 'A1/1' 'Pacific' No 60113 *Great Northern* stands with a down express for Newcastle on 29 August 1954. Designed by the NER's architect Thomas Prosser to replace the 1841 York & North Midland station, work on the new through station was completed by William Peachey in 1877. Today repainting has emphasised the elegance of the rib support column spandrels, and the track layout has been simplified, leading to the removal of the two middle roads. The cleanness of electric traction now helps the whole station to appear cleaner and brighter. *BM*

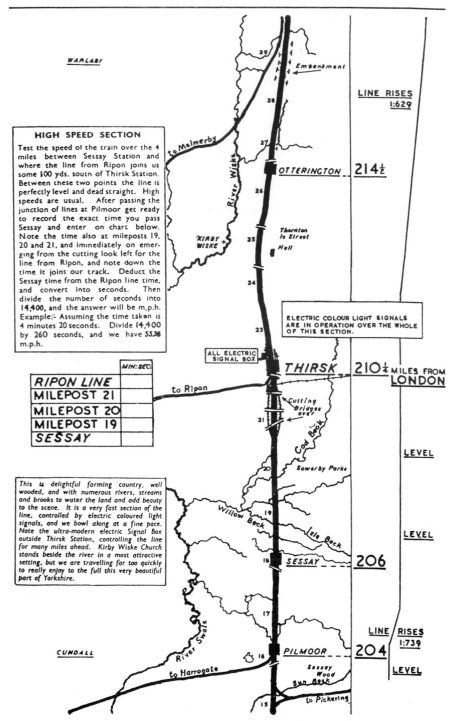

WARLABY

Embankment

LINE RISES
1:629

HIGH SPEED SECTION

Test the speed of the train over the 4 miles between Sessay Station and where the line from Ripon joins us some 100 yds. south of Thirsk Station. Between these two points the line is perfectly level and dead straight. High speeds are usual. After passing the junction of lines at Pilmoor get ready to record the exact time you pass Sessay and enter on chart below. Note the time also at mileposts 19, 20 and 21, and immediately on emerging from the cutting look left for the line from Ripon, and note down the time it joins our track. Deduct the Sessay time from the Ripon line time, and convert into seconds. Then divide the number of seconds into 14,400, and the answer will be m.p.h. Example:- Assuming the time taken is 4 minutes 20 seconds. Divide 14,400 by 260 seconds, and we have 55.38 m.p.h.

to Melmerby

River Wiske

OTTERINGTON 214½

KIRBY WISKE

Thornton le Street
Hall

ELECTRIC COLOUR LIGHT SIGNALS ARE IN OPERATION OVER THE WHOLE OF THIS SECTION.

ALL ELECTRIC SIGNAL BOX

THIRSK 210¼ MILES FROM LONDON

	MIN : SEC.
RIPON LINE	
MILEPOST 21	
MILEPOST 20	
MILEPOST 19	
SESSAY	

to Ripon

Cutting
Bridges over

Cod Beck

LEVEL

Sowerby Parks

This is delightful farming country, well wooded, and with numerous rivers, streams and brooks to water the land and add beauty to the scene. It is a very fast section of the line, controlled by electric coloured light signals, and we bowl along at a fine pace. Note the ultra-modern electric Signal Box outside Thirsk Station, controlling the line for many miles ahead. Kirby Wiske Church stands beside the river in a most attractive setting, but we are travelling far too quickly to really enjoy to the full this very beautiful part of Yorkshire.

Willow Beck

Isle Beck

LEVEL

SESSAY ---- 206

River Swale

CUNDALL

LINE RISES 1:739

PILMOOR ---- 204

to Harrogate

Sessay Wood
Sun Beck

LEVEL

to Pickering

Pilmoor to Northallerton

Continuing its straight and flat route along the fertile plain of the Vale of York, the East Coast Main Line comes to an area of former branch lines. The first, its trackbed still visible (up), is the route that used to run east via Gilling and carry York-Pickering trains. The northern spur of the triangular junction was used by summer holiday services between the North East and Scarborough. Then a little further on is the joining point (down) of what used to be the modest Harrogate-Pilmoor line, which, even in the buoyant LNER year of 1938, had only two trains each way daily. This full of character but highly unprofitable service lasted for only two years after the railway system was nationalised in 1948. The main line itself was a different matter, a section giving much pride to the old North Eastern Railway, which installed automatic semaphore signals along here as early as 1903-5.

The wide valley of the Ouse, used also by the A1 and A19 roads as well as the railway main line, is now growing narrower. Soon the Swale will be the main waterway companion and then the Wiske, as the hills on either side reduce the level stretch between first to a width of 12 miles or so at Thirsk, then even narrower at Northallerton. To the west the heights are the Pennine backbone of northern England, while east lie the Hambleton Hills with the North Yorkshire Moors beyond.

Both Thirsk and Northallerton featured in the plans of the Leeds & Thirsk Railway, later the Leeds Northern. The aim was to build a route from the West Riding to the North East, starting at Harrogate and heading north-east towards the East Coast Main Line. The principal connecting point alternated between Thirsk and Northallerton, eventually opting for the latter.

Thirsk's original L&T station, lying nearer the town than the main-line one, eventually became a good depot. The town itself lost its castle in the rebellion against Henry II but became important as a coaching centre and market for a wide area of an undramatic but highly pleasant part of North Yorkshire. It is also known for its racecourse and enjoys a good service from the Liverpool-Newcastle and Manchester Airport-Middlesbrough trains that call at the simple, modernised station.

A sad and significant railway accident occurred at Thirsk on 2 November 1892.

Opening and closing dates
Main line - Pilmoor closed 5.5.1958, Sessay and Otterington closed 15.9.1958.
Pilmoor-Gilling - opened 19.5.1853, closed 2.2.1953.
Pilmoor-Knaresborough - opened to Boroughbridge 17.6.1847, to Knaresborough 1.4.1875; closed 25.9.1950.
Thirsk-Melmerby - opened 5.1.1848 (goods), 1.6.1848 (passengers); closed 14.9.1959.
Harrogate-Northallerton - opened Harrogate-Thirsk 9.7.1849, to Northallerton 2.6.1852; closed 6.3.1967.

THIRSK: Benefiting from the gentle down gradient from Northallerton, this Newcastle-Colchester cross-country express has built up a fair speed as its passes through Thirsk station on 21 May 1959. At the leading end 'V2' Class 2-6-2 No 60812 has caught the eye of some of the train-spotters on the down platform.

Having been converted to two islands when the main line was quadrupled, a more recent rebuilding has abandoned the platform faces giving access to the main lines. Thirsk thus now has platforms to the two Slow lines only, with fences erected to protect passengers from the high speeds achieved by present-day express services passing on the main lines. One of these, the 08.00 Glasgow Central to King's Cross, is pictured on 31 August 1994. *Both BM*

After a day of worrying about his sick child, a signalman there fell asleep during his night turn and, waking suddenly, overlooked the goods train he had accepted and cleared his signals for a following express. In the collision that followed ten people died. Speed was also evident on 12 June 1973, but with a happier outcome. Near milepost 25 (from York) a prototype HST set completed a series of high-speed runs with a record-breaking 143.2 mph.

The next main-line stretch through the former station at Otterington is marked only by a series of crossings and the Fast-Slow line connections at Avenue Junction. Then the old Leeds Northern trackbed approaches (down) via a crossing of the Wiske and joins where the ECML Slow line drops down to become part of the route around the west side of Northallerton station and on to Eaglescliffe and Stockton.

The up direction link from those places passes beneath the main line and joins at Longlands Junction.

PILMOOR: On the high-speed stretch through Pilmoor it is now difficult to spot the remains of the former station and its junctions with the Knaresborough and Pickering/Malton lines. In pre-electrification days, on 13 June 1974, a block train of BRT wagons heads north behind Class 45 'Peak' No 50 (later 45040) *The King's Shropshire Light Infantry.* **A signal box and trailing crossover appear in the distance, but only quadruple plain track remains today, along with the up-side houses.** *BM*

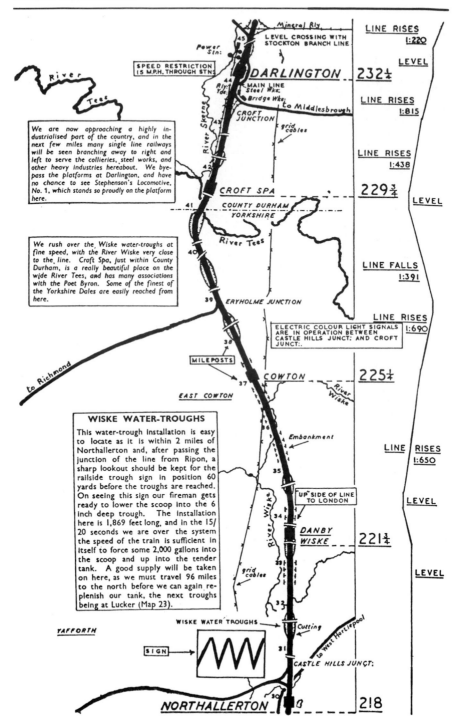

Mineral Rly

LINE RISES 1:220

LEVEL CROSSING WITH
STOCKTON BRANCH LINE

Power Stn:

SPEED RESTRICTION
15 M.P.H. THROUGH STN:

DARLINGTON — 232¼

LEVEL

MAIN LINE
Steel Wks.

River Tyd:

Bridge Wks.

To Middlesbrough

LINE RISES 1:815

CROFT JUNCTION

grid cables

River Skerne

LINE RISES 1:438

We are now approaching a highly industrialised part of the country, and in the next few miles many single line railways will be seen branching away to right and left to serve the collieries, steel works, and other heavy industries hereabout. We bypass the platforms at Darlington, and have no chance to see Stephenson's Locomotive, No. 1, which stands so proudly on the platform here.

CROFT SPA — 229¾

COUNTY DURHAM
YORKSHIRE

LEVEL

River Tees

We rush over the Wiske water-troughs at fine speed, with the River Wiske very close to the line. Croft Spa, just within County Durham, is a really beautiful place on the wide River Tees, and has many associations with the Poet Byron. Some of the finest of the Yorkshire Dales are easily reached from here.

LINE FALLS 1:391

ERYHOLME JUNCTION

LINE RISES 1:690

ELECTRIC COLOUR LIGHT SIGNALS
ARE IN OPERATION BETWEEN
CASTLE HILLS JUNCT: AND CROFT
JUNCT:.

To Richmond

MILEPOSTS

COWTON — 225¼

EAST COWTON

River Wiske

WISKE WATER-TROUGHS

This water-trough installation is easy to locate as it is within 2 miles of Northallerton and, after passing the junction of the line from Ripon, a sharp lookout should be kept for the railside trough sign in position 60 yards before the troughs are reached. On seeing this sign our fireman gets ready to lower the scoop into the 6 inch deep trough. The installation here is 1,869 feet long, and in the 15/20 seconds we are over the system the speed of the train is sufficient in itself to force some 2,000 gallons into the scoop and up into the tender tank. A good supply will be taken on here, as we must travel 96 miles to the north before we can again replenish our tank, the next troughs being at Lucker (Map 23).

Embankment

LINE RISES 1:650

UP SIDE OF LINE
TO LONDON

LEVEL

**DANBY
WISKE** — 221¼

River Wiske

grid cables

LEVEL

TAFFORTH

WISKE WATER TROUGHS

Cutting

To West Hartlepool

SIGN →

CASTLE HILLS JUNCT:

NORTHALLERTON — 218

Northallerton to Darlington

The remodelled station at Northallerton serves the administrative centre of North Yorkshire, enjoying the same cross-country services as Thirsk plus calls by East Coast Main Line expresses. The town itself dates back to Saxon times and emerged from the devastation of both Normans and Scots to become a thriving business and administrative centre, albeit today without its former railway workshops.

The once extensive service from Harrogate and on to Stockton and the Hartlepool/Sunderland route has gone, but the line remains open. It runs west of the main line station and underneath the major route just north thereof, with a connection down from High to East Junction. Slightly further on is the surviving connection (down) to the Hawes line at Castle Hills Junction. Although this isolated cross-country line closed to passengers in 1954 it remained opened for freight and until fairly recently carried limestone for British Steel from Redmire Quarry plus some passenger excursions.

Danby Wiske takes its name from the River Wiske, but the station lost its passenger trains back in 1958 and the water troughs became redundant with the advent of diesel traction for main-line expresses from 1958. On 21 June of that year D201 made history with the first diesel-electric locomotive working of the 'Flying Scotsman' service. To the east of Danby is the site of the 1138 Battle of the Standard, a major conflict in the succession quarrel between Stephen and Matilda.

There are still some platform remains at Eryholme Junction where the branch line to Richmond set off on a 10-mile journey westwards. On the way it served Catterick Bridge, well remembered by many an army trainee on his way to Catterick Camp. The line was also the scene of early experiments with train automatic warning systems. The branch service called at Croft Spa on the main line, a location once noted for its waters and for connections with Lewis Carroll and George Hudson.

Croft is also significant in railway terms for the 1829 branch of the pioneer Stockton & Darlington Railway, which linked the S&D main line with the River Tees. This was later purchased for partial incorporation in the main line and is thus its earliest section. The main line itself crosses the River Tees here, the waterway

---

Opening and closing dates

Main line - Danby Wiske and Cowton closed 15.9.1958, Croft Spa 3.3.1969.
Northallerton-Eaglescliffe - opened 2.6.1852, closed 30.8.1980.
Northallerton-Hawes - opened to Leyburn 24.11.1855 (goods), 19.5.1856 (passengers), and on to Hawes 1.6.1878 (goods), 1.10.1878 (passengers); closed 26.4.1954.
Richmond branch - opened 10.9.1846, closed 3.3.1969.
Darlington-Middlesbrough - opened (S&D) 27.12.1830, present route 1.7.1887.

DARLINGTON: During the 'Deltic' era the 09.12 Newcastle to King's Cross departs from Darlington hauled by No 55011 *Royal Northumberland Fusiliers* on 13 June 1974. Behind the train are the three great roof arches of Darlington station, supported by outer brick screen walls and by Corinthian iron columns on the central island platform. The main lines pass around the east side of the station, which dates from 1887 with a two-part restoration in the 1980s.

With Class 91 No 91005 *Royal Air Force Regiment* out of sight at the rear, the 10.00 Glasgow Central-King's Cross InterCity 225 departs from Darlington on 29 August 1994 with Mk IV DVT No 82230 leading. *Both BM*

also acting as the boundary between North Yorkshire and County Durham with lineside signs at river level to record this.

At South Junction, Darlington, the main line is joined by the route from Saltburn, which passes through the station, then continues on to Bishop Auckland. For part of the way it uses the course of the original Stockton & Darlington Railway, which opened in 1825 for the movement of coal from West Durham to the River Tees at Stockton. The first stop on this route after the main-line station is Darlington North Road, opened by the S&D in 1842 and with its yard and buildings now used as a Museum and Railway Centre. But Darlington's once notable railway works has now gone.

Returning to the main-line station, this consists of three great spans covering a centre island with bays and the main-line platform faces on either side. Darlington Bank Top, as it used to be called, was opened in 1887 to the designs of the NER architect William Bell. It still offers much of interest including the decorated Corinthian columns, the great bell from the Victoria Road clock tower, cast by John Warner & Sons of London in 1886 and now mounted on the down platform, and the S&D history panels designed by members of Hartlepool College of Art.

Avoiding lines pass around the east side of Bank Top station and rejoin at North Junction, which is followed by the departure of the Bishop Auckland line at Parkgate Junction. Gone are the former loco shed and the third of the main line's flat crossings, but the site of the latter, again part of the original S&D route, is signed.

DARLINGTON: On the up lines around the east side of Darlington station Class 'A2/3' 'Pacific' No 60512 Steady Aim restarts a full load on 20 May 1959 after getting a signal check. The locomotive is at the head of the 'Aberdeen Fish', a notable and important freight service run at Class C speeds so as not to delay the load of fish freshly caught by the Scottish fishing fleet. The boxes of iced herring and other fish needed to arrive at King's Cross for cartage to Billingsgate market early enough to ensure the best prices. BM

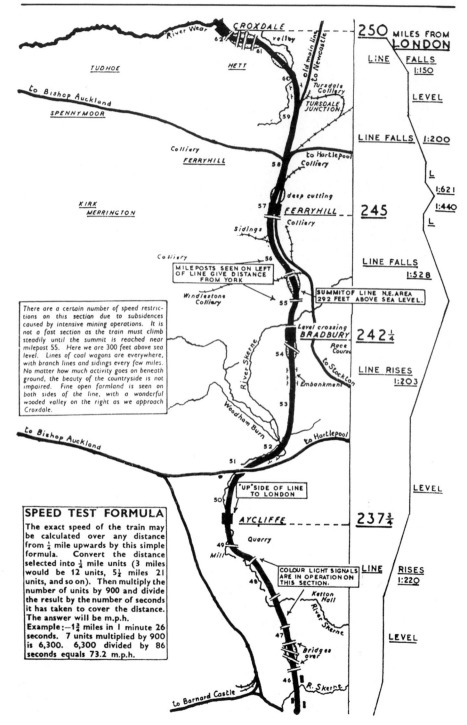

250 MILES FROM LONDON

LINE FALLS 1:150

LEVEL

LINE FALLS 1:200

L

1:621

1:440

L

245

LINE FALLS 1:528

SUMMIT OF LINE N.E. AREA
292 FEET ABOVE SEA LEVEL.

242¼

LINE RISES 1:203

LEVEL

237¾

LINE RISES 1:220

LEVEL

CROXDALE

TUDHOE

HETT

To Bishop Auckland

SPENNYMOOR

Tursdale Colliery

TURSDALE JUNCTION

Colliery FERRYHILL

to Hartlepool Colliery

KIRK MERRINGTON

deep cutting

FERRYHILL Colliery

Sidings

Colliery

MILEPOSTS SEEN ON LEFT
OF LINE GIVE DISTANCE
FROM YORK

Windlestone Colliery

Level crossing BRADBURY

Race Course

to Stockton

Embankment

To Bishop Auckland

to Hartlepool

"UP" SIDE OF LINE
TO LONDON

AYCLIFFE

Quarry

Mill

COLOUR LIGHT SIGNALS
ARE IN OPERATION ON
THIS SECTION.

Ketton Hall

Bridges over

R. Skerne

to Barnard Castle

River Wear

River Skerne

Woodham Burn

River Skerne

There are a certain number of speed restrictions on this section due to subsidences caused by intensive mining operations. It is not a fast section as the train must climb steadily until the summit is reached near milepost 55. Here we are 300 feet above sea level. Lines of coal wagons are everywhere, with branch lines and sidings every few miles. No matter how much activity goes on beneath ground, the beauty of the countryside is not impaired. Fine open farmland is seen on both sides of the line, with a wonderful wooded valley on the right as we approach Croxdale.

SPEED TEST FORMULA

The exact speed of the train may be calculated over any distance from ¼ mile upwards by this simple formula. Convert the distance selected into ¼ mile units (3 miles would be 12 units, 5½ miles 21 units, and so on). Then multiply the number of units by 900 and divide the result by the number of seconds it has taken to cover the distance. The answer will be m.p.h.
Example:—1¾ miles in 1 minute 26 seconds. 7 units multiplied by 900 is 6,300. 6,300 divided by 86 seconds equals 73.2 m.p.h.

Darlington to Croxdale

On 15 April 1844 the Newcastle & Darlington Junction Railway opened a freight line from Parkgate Junction, Darlington, through Ferryhill and on to join the Durham Junction Railway at Rainton Crossing. On 18 June the line was first used for passenger traffic and great was the excitement when a special 'flying train' carried the morning newspapers from Euston to Gateshead in 8 hours 11 minutes, averaging 37 mph for the 303 miles involved. The special reached York via Normanton, passed over the 1841 main line to Darlington and continued over the new 1844 line, which is still followed by today's expresses to a point just north of Ferryhill. From there the original service continued to Shincliffe, Leamside and Washington and arrived in Gateshead from the east over the route of the 1839 Brandling Junction Railway.

Leaving Darlington today via the site of the former flat crossing of the S&D route, the East Coast Main Line picks up the course of the River Skerne, then passes below the A1(M) in the first of three such encounters. Just before the second crossing of river and motorway are traces of the overbridge route of the former Clarence Railway from Sim Pasture Junction on the Stockton & Darlington line (near Newton Aycliffe) to Port Clarence, near Haverton Hill. This originated as a scheme to relieve the S&D of some of its coal haulage revenues by creating a short-cut, but overlooked the fact that the S&D controlled the first section of the route and could penalise rival traffic. In later years the line was electrified to expedite the movement of coal from West Durham to the Newport yards at Middlesbrough.

The Clarence Railway also built the line from what are now Norton Junctions, near Stockton, to Ferryhill, and this is visible (up) on the main-line approach to the Ferryhill complex with a 'Stockton' sign by the lineside for those who may be in doubt.

Feeder stations have appeared by the lineside all the way up from King's Cross,

---

Opening and closing dates
Main line - original route opened to Rainton Crossing 15.4.1844 (goods), 18.6.44 (passengers), to Washington 24.8.1838 (goods), 9.3.1840 (passengers), to Pelaw 1.9.1849 (goods), 1.10.1850 (passengers) and to Gateshead 5.9.1839; closed Ferryhill-Leamside 28.7.1941, Leamside-Sunderland 4.5.1964. Later route opened Tursdale Junction to Relly Mill Junction 15.1.1872, to Newton Hall Junction 1.4.1857, to Gateshead 2.3.1868 (goods), 1.12.1868 (passengers). Aycliffe closed 2.3.1953, Bradbury 2.1.1950, Ferryhill 6.3.1967, Croxdale 26.9.1938.
Darlington-Bishop Auckland - opened to Shildon 27.9.1825 (S&D, goods), to Bishop Auckland 8.11.1843.
Ferryhill-Stockton - opened 16.1.1834, closed 31.3.1952.
Ferryhill-Spennymoor - opened 31.3.1837 (goods), November 1845 (passengers); closed 31.3.1952.
Ferryhill-West Hartlepool - opened October 1846, closed 9.6.1952.

DARLINGTON S&D CROSSING: The original course of the pioneer Stockton & Darlington Railway made a flat crossing of the East Coast Main Line just north of Darlington Bank Top. At one period spurs linked the intersecting routes, but a new line from Darlington South Junction to Oak Tree Junction in 1887 allowed trains from the Bishop Auckland direction to serve both Darlington stations and avoid the right-angle crossing of the main line. Thereafter only declining goods and engineers' traffic used the direct Parkgate to Oak Tree line, which eventually closed from 21 May 1967. The S&D crossing and its signal box were still there when a summer special with the headboard 'CTAC Scottish Tours Express' was photographed on 28 August 1954. The 'B1' Class engine is so dirty that its number cannot be deciphered.

All that remains of the S&D crossing today is the lineside sign, passing which is the 05.04 Bristol Temple Meads-Newcastle InterCity HST led by Class 43 power car No 43194 on 29 August 1994. *Both BM*

one such being located near Ferryhill. They are a reminder of the not insignificant task involved in supplying current for the electrified services of the main line. The original construction scheme involved building some 30,000 mast foundations and support structures for the full King's Cross–Edinburgh route, these enabling the wiring of 1,500 route miles. Feeding this infrastructure there are now 16 incoming supply locations that take power from the grid at 25kV and feed it to 38 high-voltage switching stations. The latter are monitored by electrical control rooms at Hornsey, Doncaster and Cathcart.

North of Ferryhill and its private freight sidings (up) there is a former junction area with old routes to Coxhoe, Hartlepool and Byers Green. Then comes Tursdale Junction where the 'Old Main Line' went straight ahead, leaving today's 1872 route to curve gently east for its crossing of the River Wear at Sunderland Bridge, near the former Croxdale station. Prior to the building of the Selby Diversion this 1872 cut-off line from Ferryhill (Tursdale Junction) to the Durham-Bishop Auckland line at Relly Mill Junction was the last major change in the profile of the East Coast Main Line. There are some attractive views on this section and the one that follows as the line turns north again for its approach to Durham.

Those with keen vision might spot some old NER-style mileposts along here (down). Painted in black and white these have roundels bearing up to three 'points' denoting the quarter-mile divisions.

FERRYHILL: North of Darlington the East Coast Main Line rises via the former stations at Aycliffe and Bradbury, then descends again to Ferryhill. It is joined there by the line from Stockton to create a four-track section through the former station, which lost its passenger services on 6 March 1967. On 29 August 1994 Class 153 No 153307 is working the 13.55 train from Gateshead Metro Centre to Saltburn at the north end of the Ferryhill complex, with Thrislington Quarry in the background. From this area lines formerly radiated to Bishop Auckland, Sunderland, Hartlepool and Coxhoe, as well as the old main-line route via Leamside. *BM*

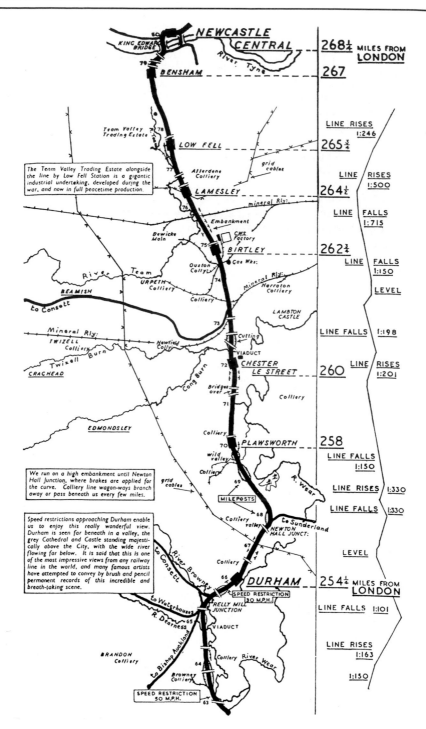

NEWCASTLE CENTRAL — 268¼ MILES FROM LONDON

KING EDWARD BRIDGE

River Tyne

BENSHAM — 267

Team Valley Trading Estate

LINE RISES 1:246

LOW FELL — 265¾

The Team Valley Trading Estate alongside the line by Low Fell Station is a gigantic industrial undertaking, developed during the war, and now in full peacetime production.

Allerdene Colliery

grid cables

LINE RISES 1:500

LAMESLEY — 264½

mineral Rly:

LINE FALLS 1:715

Embankment

Bewicke Main

CWS Factory

BIRTLEY — 262¼

Ouston Colly:

Gas Wks:

LINE FALLS 1:150

River Team

URPETH Colliery

Mineral Rly:

Harraton Colliery

LEVEL

BEAMISH

to Consett

Colliery

LAMBTON CASTLE

LINE FALLS 1:198

Mineral Rly:

TWIZELL Colliery

Burn

Newfield Colly:

Cutting

CRAGHEAD

Twizell

Cong Burn

VIADUCT

CHESTER LE STREET — 260

LINE RISES 1:201

Bridges over

Colliery

EDMONDSLEY

Colliery

PLAWSWORTH — 258

LINE FALLS 1:150

We run on a high embankment until Newton Hall Junction, where brakes are applied for the curve. Colliery line wagon-ways branch away or pass beneath us every few miles.

grid cables

wild valley

Colliery

R. Wear

LINE RISES 1:330

MILEPOSTS

LINE FALLS 1:330

Speed restrictions approaching Durham enable us to enjoy this really wonderful view. Durham is seen far beneath in a valley, the grey Cathedral and Castle standing majestically above the City, with the wide river flowing far below. It is said that this is one of the most impressive views from any railway line in the world, and many famous artists have attempted to convey by brush and pencil permanent records of this incredible and breath-taking scene.

Colliery valley

to Sunderland

NEWTON HALL JUNCT:

LEVEL

to Consett

River Browney

Colliery

DURHAM — 254¼ MILES FROM LONDON

to Waterhouses

RELLY MILL JUNCTION

SPEED RESTRICTION 30 M.P.H.

LINE FALLS 1:101

R. Deerness

VIADUCT

LINE RISES 1:163

BRANDON Colliery

to Bishop Auckland

Colliery River Wear

1:150

Browney Colliery

SPEED RESTRICTION 50 M.P.H.

Durham to Newcastle

The main line continues its scenic approach to Durham over the viaduct of the Deerness river and past the area (down) of the old Bridge House and Relly Mill junctions. Now covered with young trees, this is where the lines to Bishop Auckland, Waterhouses and Blackhill departed, their closure providing the opportunity to straighten out the previous sharp curve in the main line.

The ten-arch viaduct over the River Browney, rushing down to join the Wear (up), offers a superb view over the historic city of Durham. The viaduct was built for the 1857 Bishop Auckland branch and was incorporated in the main line when it took up its new course in 1872. As part of a round of rail improvements at Durham it has been stripped, waterproofed and relaid and its stonework cleaned along with that of the 1857 station, designed in the Tudor style probably by G. T. Andrews.

Looking out over the city ECML travellers have a fine view of the castle and cathedral that stand on a height overlooking a bend in the River Wear. The castle, begun in 1072, was a prime influence in the unsettled history of the North and became the home of the powerful prince-bishops who governed the area in the King's name. Now part of the university, the castle is slightly older than the beautiful cathedral, which was completed in 1133.

Beyond Durham longer views give way to more steep valleys after the departure (up) of the old route to Sunderland.

Through Plawsworth the line comes to Chester-le-Street, where it passes through the town on a long, 90-foot-high viaduct. To be seen (up) are the old red-brick buildings of the station and its goods shed, Lumley Castle and the more distant Lambton Castle and, on the skyline, the 'Temple of Theseus' monument to 'Radical' Jack Lambton, first Earl of Durham and first Governor of Canada.

Between Chester-le-Street and Gateshead the area used to be cut by early

Opening and closing dates
Main line - Newton Hall Junction-Gateshead opened 2.3.1868 (goods), 1.12.1868 (passengers). Plawsworth closed 7.4.1952, Birtley 5.12.1955, Lamesley 4.6.1945.
Durham-Bishop Auckland - opened 1.4.1857; closed 4.5.1964.
Durham-Waterhouses - opened 1.1.1858 (goods), 1.11.1877 (passengers); closed 29.10.1951.
Durham-Blackhill - opened to Consett 1.9.1862, to Blackhill 2.12.1867; closed 1.5.1939.
Durham-Sunderland - opened to Durham (Gilesgate) 15.4.1844 (goods), 19.6.1844 (passengers); replaced by Leamside-Bishop Auckland line 1.4.1857. Closed 4.5.1964.
Newcastle-Carlisle - opened throughout from Redheugh 18.6.1838; Tyne north bank route opened 1839-51, closed 4.10.1982 on transfer of services to south bank route.
Newcastle-Sunderland - opened to Monkwearmouth 30.8.1839 (goods), 5.9.1839 (passengers), to Sunderland 4.8.1879.

mineral lines taking coal down to the Tyne for shipment. One of the most notable, the Stanhope & Tyne, crossed and made connection with the main line just north of Chester-le-Street and in its later years carried massive trains of iron ore from Tyne Dock to Consett steelworks. The following marshalling area of Tyne Yard (down), now truncated, still handles some locomotive, wagon repair and freight activity.

Joined by the Carlisle line, the ECML now comes to the great city of Newcastle. Here the central railway layout is a great square astride the River Tyne, with the main station on the north bank of the river, the former Gateshead loco opposite and the King Edward and High Level bridges forming the other two sides. Between the latter is the Queen Elizabeth Bridge, which carries the trains of the Metro system on their journeys over former BR routes.

Newcastle station, now provided with an ultra-modern travel centre and with its track layout recently remodelled, still retains its original 1850 grandeur with majestic main buildings and great curving roof spans. Watching over the country end, where the main-line trains continue north to Edinburgh and locals head east for Sunderland, is the historic keep of the old 'New Castle', known as the Bridle of the Scots for its role in old Border conflicts.

Back in 1935 the 'Silver Jubilee' service between Newcastle and London had a 4-hour schedule. Now the 'Flying Scotsman' does the journey in 2 hours 45 minutes and will be approaching Edinburgh as the fourth hour from departure expires!

DURHAM is approached by a curving, wooded section of the route shaped by the Wear, Deerness and Browney rivers. This is followed by a high viaduct, which leads the railway round the west of the historic city and affords an impressive view of the castle and cathedral standing above a bend in the Wear. The Norman castle was the home of the Prince-Bishops of the Palatinate of Durham until 1857, which was the year that the line through Durham opened, albeit then part of the Leamside-Bishop Auckland branch. This scene was captured on 27 May 1980 with Class 37 No 37010 heading south across the viaduct with a block train load of Blue Circle cement in bulk Presflo wagons. *BM*

NEWCASTLE station was built in 1850 for the York, Newcastle & Berwick Railway with John Dobson as the architect and Robert Stephenson as engineer. Later the original three spans grew to five, the platforms to 15 and a portico was added. Like York it offers much to the interested observer, from the classical frontage and adjoining hotel to the ultra-modern travel centre on the concourse. In this pair of 'aerial' views Class 55 'Deltic' No 55002 *The King's Own Yorkshire Light Infantry* is involved in one of the many former unavoidable conflicting movements as it heads northbound from Newcastle and over the noted diamond crossings with the 05.50 King's Cross-Aberdeen.

On 30 August 1994 the 09.49 Newcastle-Morpeth train, formed of Class 142 'Pacer' No 142018, sets out on its journey across the much rationalised layout. *Both BM*

Index of locations mentioned in the text and captions